Tales from the

TERRIFIC REGISTER

—◆—

The Book of Wonders

First published 1825
This edition first published 2009

The History Press
The Mill, Brimscombe Port
Stroud, Gloucestershire, GL5 2QG
www.thehistorypress.co.uk

© Cate Ludlow, 2009

The right of Cate Ludlow to be identified as the Editor
of this work has been asserted in accordance with the
Copyrights, Designs and Patents Act 1988.

British Library Cataloguing in Publication Data.
A catalogue record for this book is available from the British Library.

ISBN 978 0 7524 5265 4

Typesetting and origination by The History Press
Printed in Great Britain

Tales from the

TERRIFIC
REGISTER

The Book of Wonders

EDITED BY
CATE LUDLOW

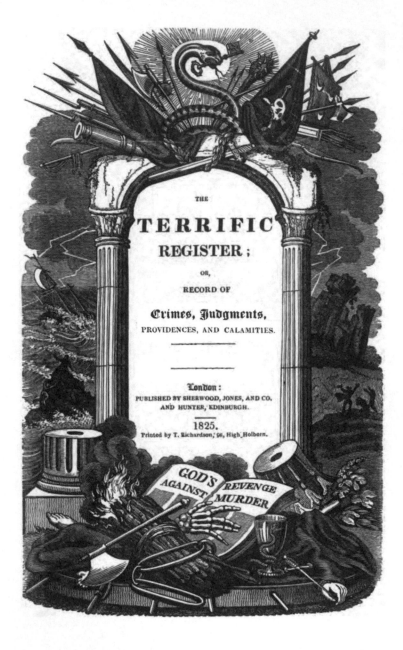

THE

TERRIFIC

REGISTER;

OR,

RECORD OF

Crimes, Judgments,

PROVIDENCES, AND CALAMITIES.

London:
PUBLISHED BY SHERWOOD, JONES, AND CO.
AND HUNTER, EDINBURGH.

1825.

Printed by T. Richardson, 98, High Holborn.

An Engagement Between A Sailor And A Shark

In the latter part of Queen Anne's reign, the sailors on board the York-Merchant, a collier, having disembarked the last part of their landing, at Barbadoes, those who had been employed in that dirty work, ventured into the sea to wash themselves, but had not been long there before a person on board observed a large shark making towards them, and gave them notice of their danger: upon which they swam back, and all but one reached the boat; him the shark overtook almost within reach of the oars, and gripping him by the small of the back, his devouring jaws soon cut him asunder, and as soon as he had swallowed the lower part of his body the remaining part was taken up, and carried on board, where his comrade was. The friendship between him and the deceased had long been distinguished by a reciprocal discharge of all such endearing offices as implied a union and sympathy of souls. On seeing the severed trunk of his friend, he was filled with horror and emotion, too great to be expressed by words. During this affecting scene, the insatiable shark was observed traversing the bloody surface, searching after the remainder of his prey. The rest of the crew thought themselves happy in being on board; he alone was unhappy, at his not being within reach of the destroyer. Fired at the sight, and vowing that he would make the devourer disgorge, or be swallowed himself, he plunged into the deep, armed with a sharp pointed knife. The shark no sooner saw him, but he made furiously towards him; both equally eager, the one for his prey, the other for revenge. The moment the shark opened his rapacious jaws, his adversary dexterously diving and grasping him with his left hand, somewhat below the upper fins, successfully employed his knife in his right hand, giving him repeated stabs in the belly. The enraged shark, after many unavailing efforts, finding himself overmatched in his own element, endeavoured to disengage himself, sometimes plunging to the bottom, then mad with pain rearing his uncouth form above the foaming waves, stained with his own streaming blood. The shark, much weakened by the loss of blood, made towards the shore, and with him his conqueror, who, flushed with an assurance of victory, pushed his foe with redoubled ardour, and by the help of an ebbing tide, dragged him on shore, ripped up his bowels, and united, and buried the severed body of his friend in one grave.

An Account Of A Family Who Were All Afflicted With the Loss Of Their Limbs

John Dowling, a poor labouring man, living at Wattisham, had a wife and six children, the eldest a girl, fifteen years of age, the youngest about four months. They were all at that time very healthy, and one of them had been ill for some time before. On Sunday the 10th of January, 1762, the eldest girl complained, in the morning, of a pain in her leg; particularly in the calf of her leg; towards the evening the pain grew exceedingly violent. The same evening, another girl complained of the same violent pain in the same leg. On the Monday, the mother and another child; and on Tuesday, all the rest of the family were afflicted in the same manner, some in one leg and some in both legs. The little infant was taken from the mother's breast; it seemed to be in pain, but the limbs did not mortify: it lived a few weeks. The mother and the other five children continued in violent pain a considerable time. In about four or five days, the diseased leg began to turn black gradually, appearing at first covered with blue spots, as if it had been bruised. The other leg of those who were affected at first only in one leg about that time was also affected with the same excruciating pain, and in a few days the leg also began to mortify. The mortified parts separated gradually from the sound parts, and the surgeon had, in most of the cases, no trouble other than to cut through the bone, which was black and almost dry. The state of the limbs was thus: Mary, the mother, aged 40 years, has lost the right foot at the ankle; the left foot is also cut off, and the two bones of the leg remain almost dry, with only some little putrid flesh adhering in the same places. The flesh is sound to about two inches below the knee. The bones would have been sawn through that place, if she would have consented to it.

Mary, aged fifteen years, both legs off below the knees – Elizabeth, aged thirteen years, both legs off below the knees.

Sarah, aged ten years, one foot off at the ankle: the other foot was affected, but not in so great a degree, and was now sound again.–Robert, aged eight, both legs off below the knees.– Edward, aged four years, both feet off.– An infant, four months old, dead.

The father was attacked about a fortnight after the rest of the family, and in a slight degree; the pain being confined to his fingers. Two fingers of the right hand continued for a long time discoloured, and partly shrunk and contracted; but he subsequently had some use of them.– The nails of the other hand were also discoloured; he lost two of them.

It is remarkable, that during all the time of this misfortune, the whole family are said to have appeared well, in other respects, ate heartily, and slept well when the violence of the pain began to abate. The mother was quite emaciated, and had very little use of her hands. The eldest girl had a superficial ulcer in one thigh. The rest of the family were pretty well. The stumps of some of them perfectly healed.

A Brand From The Burning

John Wesley's favourite phrase, that 'he was a brand plucked out of the burning', had a literal as well as a figurative meaning. Mr Wesley's father was rector of Ebworth, a market-town in the Lindsay division of Lincolnshire, irregularly built, and containing at that time in its parish about two thousand persons. The inhabitants are chiefly employed in the culture and preparation of hemp and flax, in spinning these articles, and in the manufactory of sacking and bagging. Mr Wesley found his parishioners in a profligate state; and the zeal with which he discharged his duty in admonishing them of their sins, excited a spirit of diabolical hatred in those whom it failed to reclaim. Some of these wretches twice attempted to set his house on fire, without success: they succeeded in a third attempt. At midnight some pieces of burning wood fell from the roof upon the bed in which one of the children lay, and burnt her feet. Before she could give the alarm, Mr Wesley was roused by a cry of fire from the street: little imagining it was his own house, he opened the door, and found it full of smoke, and that the roof was already burnt through. His wife being ill at the time, slept apart from him, and in a separate room. Bidding her and the eldest two girls rise and shift for their lives, he burst open the nursery-door, where the maid was sleeping with five children. He snatched up the youngest, and bade the others follow her; the eldest three did so, but John, who was then six years old, was not awakened by all this, and in the alarm and confusion he was forgotten.

By the time they reached the hall, the flames has spread every where around them, and Mr Wesley then found that the keys of the house-door were above stairs. He ran and recovered them, a minute before the staircase took fire. When the door was opened, a strong north-east wind drove in the flames with such violence from the side of the house, that it was impossible to stand against them. Some of the children got through the windows, and others through a little door, into the garden. Mrs Wesley could not reach the garden-door, and was not in a condition to climb to the window: after three times attempting to face the flames, and shrinking as often from their force, she besought Christ to preserve her, if it was his will, from that dreadful death: she then, to use her own expression, 'waded' through the fire, and escaped into the street naked as she was, with some slight scorching of the hands and face.

At this time John, who had not been remembered 'til that moment, was heard crying in the nursery. The father ran to the stairs, but they were so nearly consumed, that they could not bear his weight, and being utterly in despair, he fell upon his knees in the hall, and in agony commended the soul of the child to God. John had been awakened by the light, and thinking it was day, called to the maid to take him up; but as no one answered, he opened the curtains, and saw streaks of fire upon the top of the room. He ran to the door, and finding it impossible to escape that way, climbed upon a chest which stood near the window, and he was then seen from the yard. There was no time for procuring a ladder, but it was happily a low house; one man was hoisted upon the shoulders of another, and could then reach the window, so as to take him out: a moment later and it would have been too late: the whole roof fell in, and had it not fell inward, they must have all been crushed together. When the child was carried out to the house where his parents were, the father cried out, 'Come, neighbours, let us kneel down; let us give thanks to God! He has given me all my eight children; let the house go, I am rich enough.' John Wesley remembered this providential deliverance through life with the deepest gratitude. In reference to it he had a house in flames engraved as an emblem under one of his portraits, with these words for the motto, 'Is not this a brand plucked from the burning?'

The Awful Death of Mr Munro

This dreadful event is thus related in a letter from a friend of the unfortunate gentleman, dated December 23, 1792.

'To describe the awful, horrid, and lamentable accident I have just been an eye-witness of, is impossible. Yesterday morning, Mr Downey, of the Company's troops, Lieutenant Pyefinch, and poor Mr Munro and I, went on shore on Saugur Island, to shoot deer; we saw innumerable tracks of tygers and deer, but still we were induced to pursue our sport, and did the whole day; about half past three we sat down on the jungle to eat some cold meat sent us from the

ship, and had just commenced our meal, when Mr Pyefinch and a black servant told us there was a fine deer within six yards of us; Mr Downey and I immediately jumped up to take our guns – mine was the nearest; and I had just laid hold of it, when I heard a roar like thunder, and saw an immense royal tyger spring on the unfortunate Munro, who was sitting down; in a moment his head was in the beast's mouth, and he rushed into the jungle with him with as much ease as I could lift a kitten, tearing him through the thickest bushes and trees – every thing yielding to his monstrous strength. The agonies of horror, regret, and I must say fear, (for there were two tygers, a male and a female), rushed on me at once; the only effort I cold make was to fire at him, though the poor youth was still in his mouth. I relied partly on Providence, partly on my own aim, and fired a musket. I saw the tyger stagger and agitated, and I cried out so immediately; Mr Downey then fired two shots, and I one more. We retired from the jungle, and a few minutes after, Mr Munro came up to us, all over blood, and fell; we took him on our backs to the boat, and got every medical assistance for him from the Valentine Indiaman, which lay at anchor near the island, but in vain. He lived twenty-four hours in the extreme of torture: his head and scull were all torn and broken to pieces, and he was wounded by the beast's claws all over his neck and shoulders: but it was better to take him away, though irrecoverable, than leave him to be devoured limb by limb. We have just read the funeral service over his body, and committed it to the deep. He was an amiable and promising youth.

'I must observe there was a large fire blazing close to us, composed of ten or a dozen whole trees: I made it myself on purpose to keep the tygers off, as I had always heard it would. There were eight or ten of the natives about us; many shots had been fired at the place, and much noise and laughing at the time, but the ferocious animal disregarded all.

'The human mind cannot form an idea of the scene: it turned my very soul within me. The beast was about four feet and a half high, and nine long. His head first appeared as large as an ox's, his eyes darting fire, and his roar, when he first seized his prey, will never be out of my recollection. We had scarcely pushed our boat from that cursed shore, when the tygress made her appearance, raging mad almost, and remained on the sand as long as the distance would allow me to see her.'

The Guardian Snake

On a journey from Baroche to Dhuboy, a Mr Forbes stopped at Nurrah, a large ruined town, which had been plundered and burnt by the Mahrattas. The principle house had belonged to an opulent man, who emigrated during the war, and died in a distant country. Mr Forbes was privately informed that under one of the towers there was a secret cell, formed to contain his treasure; the information could not be doubted, because it came from the mason, who constructed the cell. Accordingly, the man accompanied him through several spacious courts and apartments, to a dark closet in that tower; the room was about eight feet square, being the whole size of the interior of the tower; and it was some stories above the place where the treasure was said to be deposited. In the floor there was a hole large enough for a slender person to pass through: they enlarged it and sent two men down by a ladder. After descending several feet, they came to another floor, composed in a like manner of bricks and channam, and here also was a similar aperture. This also was enlarged, torches were procured, and by their light Mr Forbes perceived from the upper apartment a dungeon of great depth below, as the mason had described.

He desired the men to descend and search for the treasure; but they refused, declaring that wherever the money was concealed in Hindostan, there was also a demon, in the shape of a serpent, to guard it. He laughed at their superstition, and repeated his orders in such a manner as to enforce obedience, though his attendants sympathised with the men, and seemed to expect the event with more of fear and awe than of curiosity. The ladder was too short to reach the dungeon; strong ropes therefore were sent for, and more torches. The men reluctantly obeyed, and as they were lowered, the dark sides and the moist floor of the dungeon extinguished the light which they carried in their hands. But they had not been many seconds on the ground, before they screamed out that they were enclosed with a large snake. In spite of their screams, Mr Forbes was incredulous, and declared that the ropes should not be let down until he had seen the creature; their cries were dreadful; he however was inflexible; and the upper lights were held steadily, to give him as distinct as view as possible into the dungeon. There he perceived something like billets of wood, or rather, he says, like a ship's cable seen from the deck, coiled up in a dark hole; but no language can express his sensation of astonishment and terror, when he saw a serpent actually rear his head over an immense length of body, coiled in volumes on the ground, and working itself into an exertion by a sort of sluggish motion. 'What I felt,' he continues, 'on seeing two fellow-creatures exposed by my orders to this fiend, I must leave to the reader's imagination.' To his inexpressible joy they were drawn up unhurt, but almost lifeless with fear.

Hay was then thrown down upon the lighted torches which they had dropped.– When the flames had expired, a large snake was found scorched and dead, but no money. Mr Forbes supposes that the owner had carried away the treasure with him, but forgotten to liberate the snake placed there as its keeper. Whether the snake was venomous or not, he has omitted to mention, or perhaps to observe; if he were not, it would be no defence for the treasure: and if it were, it seems to have become too torpid with inaction, confinement, and darkness, to exercise its powers of destruction. Where the popular beliefs prevails that snakes are the guardians of hidden treasure, and where the art of charming serpents is commonly practiced, there is no difficulty in supposing that they who conceal a treasure (as is frequently done under the oppressive government of the East) would sometimes place it under such protection.

Horrors Of The Plague At Marseilles, 1720

Which way soever one turns, the streets appear strowed on both sides with dead bodies close by each other, most of which being putrefied, are insupportably hideous to behold.

As the numbers of slaves employed to take them out of the houses, is very insufficient to be able to carry all off daily, some frequently remain there whole weeks; and would remain longer, if the stench they emit, which poisons the neighbours, did not compel them for their own preservation, to overcome all aversion to such horrid work, and go into the apartments where they lie, to drag them down into the streets: they pull them out with hooks, and hawl them by ropes fastened to the staves of those hooks into the streets: this they do in the night, that they may draw them to some distance from their own houses; they leave them extended before another's door, who at opening it the next morning is frightened at the sight of such an object, which generally infects him and gives him death.

The Ring, and all public walks, squares, and market-places, the key of the port, are spread with dead bodies, some lying in heaps: the square before the building called the Loge, and the pallisadoes of the port, are filled with the continual number of dead bodies that are brought ashore from the ships and vessels, which are crowded with families, whom fear induced to take refuge there, in a false persuasion that he plague would not reach them upon the water.

Under every tree in the Ring and walks, under every pent-house of the shops in the streets and on the port, one sees among the dead a number of poor sick, and even whole families, lying on a little straw, or on ragged mattresses; some are in a languishing condition, to be relieved only by death; others are light-headed by the force of the venom which rages in them; they implore the assistance of those who pass by; some in pitiful complaints, some in groans and outcries, which pain or frenzy draw from them. An intolerable stink exhales from among them: they not only endure the effects of distemper, but suffer equally by the public want of food and common necessaries: they die under rags that cover them, and every moment adds to the number of the dead that lie about them. It rends the heart, to behold on the pavement so many wretched mothers, who have lying by their sides the dead bodies of their children, whom they have seen expire, without being able to give them any relief; and so many poor infants still hanging at the breasts of the mothers, who died holding them in their arms, sucking in the rest of that venom which will soon put them in the same condition.

If any space be yet left in the streets, it is filled with infected household goods and clothes, which are thrown out of windows every where, so that one cannot find a void space to set one's foot.

All the dogs and cats that are killed, lie putrefying every where among the dead bodies, the sick, and the infected clothes; all the port is filled with those thrown into it; and while they float, they add their stench to the general infection, which has spread all over the town, and preys among the vitals, the senses, and the mind.

Those one meets in the streets, are generally livid and drooping, as if their souls had begun to part from their bodies; or whom the violence of the distemper has made delirious, who wandering about they know not whither, as long as they can keep on their legs, soon drop through weakness; and, unable to get up again, expire on the spot; some writhed into strange postures, denoting the torturing venom which struck them to the heart; others are agitated by such disorders of the mind, that they cut their own throats, or leap into the sea, or throw themselves out of the window, to put an end to their misery, and prevent the death which was not far off. Nothing is to be heard or seen on all sides but distress, lamentation, tears, sighs, groans, affright, despair.

To conceive of so many horrors, one must figure to one's self, in one view, all the miseries and calamities that human nature is subject to; and one cannot venture to draw near such a scene, without being struck dead, or seized with unutterable horrors of the mind.

Intrepid Encounter With A Wolf

Wolves were very numerous at Connecticut, in the United States of America, soon after General Putnam removed thither: they broke into a sheep fold, and killed upwards of seventy fine sheep and goats, besides wounding many others. This havoc was committed by an old she-wolf, which, with her annual whelps, had for many years been obnoxious in the country. The young were commonly destroyed by the vigilance of the hunters; but the old one was too sagacious to come within gun-shot. Upon being closely pursued, she would generally fly to the western woods, and return the following winter with another litter of whelps.

This wolf became, at length, such an intolerable nuisance, that Mr Putnam entered into a combination with five of his neighbours to hunt alternately until they could destroy her. Two, by rotation, were to be constantly in pursuit. It was known that, having lost the toes from one foot, by a steel trap, she made one track shorter than the other. By this vestige, the pursuers recognised, in a light snow, the route of this ferocious animal. Having followed her to Connecticut river, and found that she had turned back in a direct course towards Pomfref, they immediately returned, and by ten the next morning, the blood-hounds had driven her into a den about three miles distant from the house of Mr Putnam; the people soon collected with dogs, guns, straw, fire, and sulphur to attack the common enemy. With this apparatus, several unsuccessful efforts were made to force her from the den. The hounds came back badly wounded, and refused to return. The smoke of the blazing straw had no effect, nor did the fumes of burnt brimstone, with which the cavern was filled, compel her to quit the retirement. Wearied with such fruitless attempts (which had brought the time to ten o'clock at night), Mr Putnam tried once more to make his dog enter; but in vain: he proposed his man to go down into the cavern, and shoot the

wolf; he declined the hazardous service. Then it was, that the General, angry at his disappointment, and declaring that he was ashamed to have a coward in his family, resolved himself to destroy the ferocious beast, lest she should escape through some unknown fissure of the rock. His neighbours strongly remonstrated against the perilous enterprise; but he, knowing that wild animals were intimidated by fire, had provided several strips of birch-bark, the only combustible material which he could obtain that would afford light in the darksome cave, prepared for his descent.

Having, accordingly, divested himself of his coat and waistcoat, and having a long rope fastened to his legs, by which he might be pulled out at a concerted signal, he entered, head foremost, with a blazing torch in his hand. The aperture of the den, on the east side of a very high ledge of rocks, is about two feet square: from thence it descends obliquely fifteen feet, then running horizontally about ten more, it descends gradually sixteen feet towards its termination. The sides of this subterraneous cavity are composed of smooth and solid rocks, which seem to have been divided from each other by some former earthquake. The top and bottom are also of stone, and the entrance in the winter being covered with ice, is exceedingly slippery. It is no place high enough for a man to raise himself upright, nor in any part more than three feet in width. Having groped his passage to the horizontal part of the den, the most terrifying darkness appeared in front of the dim circle of light afforded by his torch. It was silent as the house of death: none but monsters of the desert have ever before explored this solitary mansion of horror. He, cautiously proceeding onward, came to the ascent, which he slowly mounted, on his hands and knees, until he discovered the glaring eyeballs of the wolf, who was sitting at the extremity of the cavern. Startled at the sight of fire, she gnashed her teeth, and gave a sudden growl. As soon as he had made the necessary discovery, he kicked the rope as a signal for pulling him out. The people of the mouth of the den, who had listened with painful anxiety, hearing the growling of the wolf, and supposing their friend to be in the utmost danger, drew him forth with such celerity, that his shirt was stripped over his head, and his skin severely lacerated.

After he had adjusted his cloths, and loaded his gun with nine buck-shot, holding a torch in one hand, and the musket in the other, he descended a second time. When he drew nearer than before, the wolf, assuming a still more fierce and terrible appearance, howling, rolling her eyes, snapping her teeth, and dropping her head between her legs, was evidently in the attitude, and on the point of springing at him. At the critical instant he levelled and fired at her head. Stunned with the shock, and suffocated with the smoke, he immediately found himself drawn out of the cave. But having refreshed himself, and permitted the smoke to dissipate, he went down a third time; once more he came within sight of the wolf who appeared very passive; he applied the torch to her nose, and, perceiving her dead, he took hold of her ears, and then kicking the rope (still tied around his legs), the people above, with no small exultation, dragged them both out together.

Singular Preservation

When the rapid and dreadful conflagration happened on board the Boyne a marine was peaceably sitting in his birth with his wife and son, a boy about twenty months old, just beneath the place where the misfortune began, and finding every effort to escape the flames in the ordinary way ineffectual, the man with the greatest composure and presence of mind, took from the pens a sheep of the captain's livestock, and bracing the boy on the animal's fleecy back, dropped them into the sea. 'There,' said he, 'turn to the land, and God be with you.' Encouraged by her husband's resolution, his wife leaped into the brine, and the man followed after, supporting his companion above water, till the boats arrived to their assistance, when they were taken up, little worse for the venture. The sheep with the greatest steadiness, was seen making for the shore, with young Ben Bowline riding upon his back like an infant river-god, to the vast delight of the spectators on shore, who, from the tenderest motives, finding themselves interested in the boy's safety, rushed into the watery element to meet the young navigator, whom they presently unsheeped, and succoured with tenderness, till he again fell into the arms of his adventurous parents.

The Combat Of The Dog Of Montargis
With The Assassin Of His Master

The fame of an English dog has been deservedly transmitted to posterity by a monument in basso relievo, which still remains on the chimney-piece of the grand hall, at the castle of Montargis in France. The sculpture, which represents a dog fighting with a champion, is explained by the following narrative.

Aubri de Mondidier, a gentleman of family and fortune, travelling alone through the forest of Bondi, was murdered and buried under a tree. His dog, an English blood-hound, would not quit his master's grave for several days; till at length, compelled by hunger, he proceeded to the house of an intimate friend of the unfortunate Aubri, at Paris, and by his melancholy howling, seemed desirous of expressing the loss they had both sustained. He repeated his cries, ran to the door, looked back to see if any one followed him, returned to his master's friend, pulled him by the sleeve, and with dumb eloquence entreated him to go with him.

The singularity of all these actions of the dog, added to the circumstance of his coming without his master, whose faithful companion he had always been, prompted the company to follow the animal, who conducted them to a tree, where he renewed his howl, scratching the earth with his feet, and significantly entreating them to search that particular spot. Accordingly, on digging, the body of the unfortunate Aubri was found.

Some time after, the dog accidentally met the assassin, who is styled, by all historians that relate the fact, the Chevalier Macaire; when instantly seizing him by the throat, he was with great difficulty compelled to quit his prey.

In short, whenever the dog saw the chevalier, he continued to pursue and attack him with equal fury. Such obstinate virulence in the animal, confined only to Macaire, appeared very extraordinary; especially to those who at once recollected the dog's remarkable attachment to his master, and several instances in which Macaire's envy and hatred to Aubri de Mondidier, had been conspicuous.

Additional circumstances created suspicion; and at length the affair reached the royal ear. The king (Louis VIII) accordingly sent for the dog, which appeared extremely gentle, till he perceived Macaire in the midst of several noblemen, when he ran fiercely towards him, growling and attacking him as usual.

The king, struck with such a collection of circumstantial evidence against Macaire, determined to refer the decision to the chance of battle; in other words, he gave orders for a combat between the chevalier and the dog. The lists were appointed in the isle of Notre Dame, then an unenclosed, uninhabited place, and Macaire was allowed for his weapon a great cudgel.

An empty hutch was given to the dog as a place of retreat, to enable him to recover breath. Every thing being prepared, the dog no sooner found himself at liberty, than he ran round his adversary, avoiding his blows, and menacing him on every side, till his strength was exhausted; then springing forward, he gripped him by the throat, threw him on the ground, and obliged him to confess his guilt, in the presence of the king and the whole court. In consequence of this, the chevalier, after a few days, was convicted upon his own acknowledgements and beheaded on a scaffold in the isle of Notre Dame.

Providential Escape

In the year 1709, a packet boat, returning from Holland to England, was so shaken by a tempest, that she sprung a leak, and was in the utmost extremity of danger in the midst of her course, when all the mariners and passengers were in the last distress, and the pumps had been worked to carry off the water, but all to little purpose; by a good Providence the hole filled and was stopped seemingly of itself. This struck them all with wonder and astonishment. No sooner did they get safe into port, than they examined the ship, to see what was the matter, and found a fish sticking in the very hole, which had been driven into it by the force of the tempest. Without this wonderful Providence, they must all have perished.

Grievous Famine At Sea

Captain Bradshaw, commander of the Andalusia, in a letter, dated Halifax, April 30, 1759, gave the following distressing narration:

On the 27th of February, about two o'clock in the afternoon, we saw a vessel without masts, about three miles to leeward of us; and immediately bore down to see what she was: I found it to be the Dolphin sloop, captain Baron, from the Canaries, bound to New York; they had been from the Canaries, ever since September 11th, 165 days; 115 of which they had nothing to eat. I sent my boats on board to see what condition they were in; my people called to me and told me they were helpless and starving, and desired to know whether I would take them on board.– I ordered my people to put them in the boat, and bring them on board, which accordingly they did. When they came alongside our ship we were obliged to haul them in with ropes, they were so very weak: they were the captain and seven others; but such poor miserable creatures sure never were seen: had it been a week longer they must all have died. When I came to examine the captain and the people, they told me, that they had eaten their dog, their cats, and all their shoes, and, in short, every thing that was eatable on board. On the 10th of January they all agreed to cast lots for their lives, which accordingly they did; the shortest lot was to die; the next shortest to be the executioner. The lot fell upon Anthony Gallitia, a Spanish gentleman, a passenger; they shot him through the head, which they cut off and threw overboard; they then took out his bowels and ate them, and afterwards ate all the remaining part of the body, which lasted but a short time. The captain told me, that they were about to cast lots for the second time, but it happened very luckily that he bethought himself of a pair of breeches, which he had lined with leather; he soon found them, took out the lining, and cut off for each man's share a piece of about an inch and a half square, for the day's allowance; that, with the grass that grew upon the deck, was all the support they had for about twenty days before I met with them: the grass was in some places four or five inches high. The captain brought on board the remaining part of the leather lining, which I have got, and a piece of the same that was the allowance of one man for the day. No words in my power to express, are sufficient to describe the truly deplorable and wretched condition these poor unfortunate sufferers were in when I met with them.

Miraculous Shot

The hero of this little narrative was a Hottentot, of the name of Von Wyhk, and we give the story of his perilous and fearful shot in his own words: 'It is now,' said he, 'more than two years since, in the very place where we stand, I ventured to take one of the most daring shots that has ever been hazarded; my wife was sitting in the house near the door, the children were playing about her. I was without, near the house, busied in doing something to a wagon, when suddenly, though it was mid-day, an enormous lion appeared, came up, and laid himself quietly down in the shade, upon the very threshold of the door. My wife, either frozen with fear, or aware of the danger attending an attempt to fly, remained motionless in her place, while the children took refuge in her lap. The cry they uttered attracted my attention, and I hastened towards the door; but my astonishment may well be conceived, when I found the entrance barred in such a manner. Although the animal had not seen me, escape, unarmed as I was, appeared impossible. Yet I glided gently, scarcely knowing what I meant to do, to the side of the house, up to the window of my chamber, where I knew my loaded gun was standing. By a happy chance, I had set it in a corner close to the window, so that I could reach it with my hand; for the opening being too small to admit of my having got in; and still more fortunately, the door of the room was open, so that I could see the whole danger of the scene. The lion was beginning to move, perhaps with the intention of making a spring: I called softly to the mother not to be afraid, and invoking the name of the Lord, fired my piece. The ball passed directly over my boy's head, and entered the forehead of the lion, immediately above his eyes, which shot forth as it were sparks of fire, and stretched him on the ground, so that he never stirred more.'

Dreadful Conflict With A Serpent

In the fourteenth century, an amphibious animal, a sort of serpent or crocodile, caused much disorder in the Island of Rhodes by its depredations, and several inhabitants fell victims to its rapacity. The retreat of this animal was in a cavern, situated near a morass at the foot of Mount St. Etienne, two miles from Rhodes. It often came out to seek its prey, and devoured sheep, cows, horses, and even shepherds who watched over the flocks.

Many of the Knights of St John of Jerusalem had essayed to destroy this monster; but they never returned. This induced Phelion de Villenueve, the grand master of Malta, to forbid all knights, on pain of being deprived of their habit, from attacking it, or attempting any further an enterprise which appeared to be above human powers.

All the knights obeyed the mandate of the grand master, except Dieu Donne de Gozon, a native of Provence, who, notwithstanding the prohibition, and without being deterred by the fate of his brethren, secretly formed the daring design of fighting this savage beast, bravely resolving to deliver the Isle of Rhodes from such a calamity, or perish in the attempt. Having learnt that the serpent had no scales on its belly, upon that information he formed the plan of his enterprise. From the description he had received of this enormous beast, he made a wooden or pasteboard figure of it, and he endeavoured to imitate its terrific cries. He then trained two young mastiffs to run to its cries, and to attach themselves immediately to the belly of the monster; whilst he, mounted on horseback, his lance in his hand, and covered with his

armour, feigned to give it blows in several places. The knight employed himself many months, every day, in this exercise, at the Chateau de Gozon, in Languedoc, to which he had repaired; and when he had trained the mastiffs sufficiently to this kind of combat, he hastened back to Rhodes.

Having first repaired to church, and commended himself to God, he put on his armour, mounted his horse, and ordered his two servants to return to France, if he perished in the combat; but to come near him if they perceived that he had killed the serpent, and been wounded by it. He then descended from the mountain of St Etienne, and approaching the haunt of the serpent soon encountered it. Gozon struck it with his lance, but the scales prevented it taking effect.

He prepared to redouble his blows, but the horse, frightened with the hisses of the serpent, refused to advance, and threw himself on his side. Gozon dismounted, and accompanied by his mastiffs, marched sword in hand towards this horrible beast. He struck him in various places, but the scales prevented him from penetrating them. This furious animal by a blow of his tail knocked down the knight, and would

27

certainly have devoured him, had not his two dogs fastened on the belly of the serpent, which they lacerated in a dreadful manner. The knight, favoured by this help, rejoined his mastiffs, and buried his sword in the body of the monster; which being mortally wounded, rushed on the knight, and would have crushed him to death by its weight, had not his servants, who were spectators of the combat, come to his relief. The serpent was dead, and the knight had fainted. When he recovered, the first and most agreeable object which could present itself to his view, was the dead body of his enemy.

The death of the serpent was no sooner known in the city, than a crowd of the inhabitants came out to welcome their deliverer. The knights conducted him in triumph to the grand master, who, however, considered it a breach of discipline unpardonable, even on such an occasion; and regardless of the entreaties of the knights, and the important service that Gozon had rendered, sent him to prison. A council was assembled, who decided that he should be deprived of the habit of his order for his disobedience. This was done; but Villeneuve repenting of his severity, soon restored him, and loaded him with favours.

Nothing could exceed the joy of the inhabitants in being delivered from this monster, whose head they stuck on one of the gates of the city, as a monument of the victory of Gozon, whom they regarded as their deliverer.

Resurrection And Subsequent Felicity

Many who were personally acquainted with Professor Junker, have frequently heard him relate the following anecdote:

Being professor of anatomy, he once procured, for dissection, the bodies of two criminals who had been hanged. The key of the dissecting-room not being at hand when they were brought home to him, he ordered them to be laid down in an apartment which opened onto his bed-chamber. The evening came, and Junker, according to custom, proceeded to resume his literary labours before he retired to rest. It was now near midnight, and all his family were fast asleep, when he heard a rumbling noise in his closet. Thinking that by some mistake the cat had been shut up with the dead bodies, he rose, and taking the candle, went to see what had happened. But what must have been his astonishment, or rather his panic, on perceiving that the sack, which contained the two bodies, was rent through the middle? He approached, and found that one of them was gone.

The doors and windows were well secured, and that the body could have been stolen, he thought impossible. He tremblingly looked round the closet, and found the dead man seated in a corner.

Junker stood for a moment motionless; the dead man seemed to look towards him: he moved both to the right and left, but the dead man still kept his eyes fixed on him.

The Professor then retired, step by step, with his eyes still fixed on the object of alarm, and holding the candle in his hand until he reached the door. The dead man instantly started up, and followed him. A figure of so hideous an appearance, naked, and in motion, the lateness of the hour, the deep silence which prevailed – every thing concurred to overwhelm him with confusion. He let fall the only candle which was burning, and all was darkness.

He made his escape to his apartment, and threw himself on his bed: thither, however, he was followed; and he soon found the dead man embracing his legs, and loudly sobbing.

Repeated cries of 'leave me! leave me!' released Junker from the grasp of the dead man, who now exclaimed, 'Ah! good executioner, good executioner! have mercy upon me!'

Junker soon perceived the cause of what had happened, and resumed his fortitude. He informed the re-animated sufferer who he really was, and made a motion, in order to call up some of his family. 'You then wish to destroy me,' exclaimed the criminal. 'If you call up any one, my adventure will become public, and I shall be taken and executed a second time. In the name of humanity, I implore you to save my life.'

The physician struck a light, decorated his guest with an old night-gown, and having made him drink a cordial, requested to know what had brought him to the gibbet. 'It would have been a truly singular exhibition,' observed Junker, 'to have seen me at that late hour engaged in a tête a tête with a dead man, decked out in an old night-gown.'

The poor wretch informed him, that he had enlisted as a soldier, but that, having no great attachment to the profession, he had determined to desert; that he had entrusted his secret to a kind of crimp, a fellow of no principle, who recommended him to a woman, in whose house he was to remain concealed; that this woman had discovered his retreat to the officers of the police, &c.

Junker was extremely perplexed how to save the poor man. It was impossible to retain him in his own house, and keep the affair a secret; and to turn him out of doors, was to expose him to certain destruction. He resolved to conduct him out of the city, in order that he might get him into a foreign jurisdiction; but it was necessary they pass the gates, which were strictly guarded. To accomplish this point, he dressed him in some of his old clothes, covered him with a cloak, and at an early hour, set out of the country with his protégée behind him. On arriving at the city-gate, where he was well known, he said, in a hurried tone, that he had been sent for to visit a sick person in the suburbs, who was dying. He was permitted to pass. Having both got into the fields, the deserter threw himself at the feet of his deliverer, to whom he vowed eternal gratitude; and after receiving some pecuniary assistance, departed, offering up prayers for his happiness.

Twelve years after, Junker, having occasion to go to Amsterdam, was accosted on the Exchange by a man well dressed, and of the first appearance, who, he had been informed, was one of the most respectable merchants of that city. The merchant, in a polite tone, inquired whether he was not Professor Junker, of Halle; and being answered in the affirmative, he requested, in an earnest manner, his company to dinner. The Professor consented. Having reached the merchant's house, he was shewn into an elegant apartment, where he found a beautiful wife, and two fine healthy children; but he could scarcely suppress his astonishment at meeting so cordial a reception from a family, with whom, he thought, he was entirely unacquainted.

After dinner, the merchant, taking him into his counting-room, said, 'You do not recollect me?'– 'Not at all.'– 'But I will recollect you, and never shall your features be effaced from my remembrance. You are my benefactor; I am the person who came to live in your closet, and to whom you paid so much attention. On parting from you, I took the road to Holland. I wrote a good hand; was tolerably good at accounts; my figure was somewhat interesting, and I soon obtained employment as a merchant's clerk! My good conduct and my zeal for the interests of my patron, procured me his confidence, and his daughter's love. On retiring from business, I succeeded him, and became his son-in-law. But for you, however, I should not have lived to experience all these enjoyments. Henceforth, look upon my house, my fortune, and myself, as at your disposal.' Those who possess the smallest portion of sensibility can easily represent to themselves the feelings of Junker.

Skeleton Of A Wreck

While Sir Michael Seymour was in the command of the Amethyst frigate, and was cruizing in the Bay of Biscay, the wreck of a merchant ship drove past. Her deck was just above water; her lower mast alone standing. Not a soul could be seen on board; but there was a cub-house on the deck, which had the appearance of having been recently patched with old canvass and tarpauling, as if to afford shelter to some forlorn remnant of the crew. It blew at this time a strong gale, but Sir Michael, listening only to the dictates of humanity, ordered the ship to be put about, and sent off a boat with instructions to board the wreck, and ascertain whether there was any being still surviving, whom the help of his fellow men might save from the grasp of death. The boat rowed towards a drifting mass; and while struggling with the difficulty of getting through a high running sea close alongside, the crew shouting all the time as loud as they could, an object resembling in appearance a bundle of clothes was observed to roll out of the cub-house against the lee shrouds of the mast. With the end of a boat-hook they managed to get hold of it, and hauled it to the boat, when it proved to be the trunk of a man, bent head and knees together, and so wasted away, as scarcely to be felt within the ample clothes which had once fitted it in a state of life and strength. The boat's crew hastened back to the Amethyst with this miserable remnant of mortality; and so small was it in bulk, that a lad of fourteen years of age was able with his own hands to lift it into the ship. When placed on deck, it shewed for the first time, to the astonishment of all, signs of remaining life; it tried to move and next moment muttered, in a hollow sepulchral tone, 'there is another man.'

The instant these words were heard, Sir Michael ordered the boat to shove off again for the wreck. The sea having now become somewhat smoother, they succeeded this time in boarding the wreck; and on looking into the cub-house, they found two other human bodies, wasted like the one they had saved to very bones, but without the least spark of life remaining. They were sitting in a shrunk up posture, a hand of one resting on a tin pot, in which there was about a gill of water; and a hand of the other reaching to the deck, as if to regain a bit of raw salt beef about the size of a walnut, which had dropped from its nerveless grasp. Unfortunate men! They had starved on their scanty store till they had not strength remaining to lift the last morsel to their mouths! The boat's crew having completed their melancholy survey, returned on board, where they found the attention of the ship's company engrossed by the efforts made to preserve the generous skeleton, who seemed to have just life enough to breathe the remembrance that there was still 'another man', his companion in suffering, to be saved. Captain S. committed him to the special charge of the surgeon, who spared no means which humanity or skill could suggest, to achieve the noble object of creating anew, as it were, a fellow creature, whom famine had stripped of almost every living energy. For three weeks he scarcely ever left his patient, giving him nourishment with his own hand every five or ten minutes, and at the end of three weeks more, the 'skeleton of the wreck' was seen walking on the deck of the Amethyst; and, to the surprise of all who recollected that he had been lifted into the ship by a cabin boy, presented the stately figure of a man nearly six feet high!

Murder Prevented By A Dream

A few years ago, a gentleman, whose situation in life is rather distinguished, and whose character is such as to stamp with veracity whatever he might impart, dreamed that he went down into his kitchen in the middle of the night, and found his cook sitting there alone, dressed in white, but with a large spot of blood on her bosom.

The dream caused so powerful an emotion, that he awoke, but immediately after he fell asleep, and again dreamed the same dream; he a second time awoke, and, though not superstitiously inclined, he was so deeply impressed that he felt impelled to go down, and satisfy himself by ocular demonstration, that there was no cause for uneasiness. He accordingly proceeded to the kitchen; but what was his horror, on swiftly opening the door, to perceive the cook seated by the fire, and in just such a dress as his sleeping vision had portrayed! He demanded somewhat sternly what could be her business down there at such an hour? The woman appeared much agitated at this discovery, trembled, and faltered; but, on her master's renewing his question in an authoritative tone, she acknowledged that she and the gardener had been long attached, and that he had promised to meet her at that early hour, in order to accompany her to a village some miles distant to be married. The circumstances were so odd, more especially as connected with the dream, that this gentleman felt convinced all could not be right; and, having first locked up the cook safely in the kitchen, he proceeded to a little detached building in which the gardener slept; but not finding him there, he went on to the garden, where he found him digging a pit.

He started, and turned dreadfully pale at the sight of his master, who asked him how long he had been in the habit of rising at so early an hour, and for what he was digging the pit? He answered he was preparing a melon-bed; but his looks and his voice confirmed the dreadful suspicion of the dark purpose for which it was destined, and in the most solemn manner his master charged him with intended murder. Thrown off his guard by the suddenness of this visit, and the unexpectedness of the accusation, he fell down on his knees, and, earnestly begging for pardon, acknowledged that he had powerful reasons for wishing the cook entirely out of the way, and that he had really prepared this pit for her reception!

Astonishing Instance Of Noble Generosity Of A Lion

In the early part of the seventeenth century, the menagerie of Florence contained some of the rarest specimens of animal creation, and among them a lion of untameable disposition. No caresses, no kindnesses, no favour, could render him in any way tractable. One evening, having burst the bars of the cage that held him, he leaped a window two stories high, and furiously ran through the streets of Florence, roaring in the most hideous manner, and spreading every where the utmost terror and dismay. Death and desolation followed in his track; and the people of the town secured themselves from his fury. Those of the inhabitants who happened to be in his path fled before him like chaff before the wind, and many were trampled to death, ere they had time to escape.

A woman flying from his fury with her infant in her arms, stumbled, and dropped it, when it was immediately seized by the enraged animal. Frantic at this horrible disaster, she threw herself on her knees before the lion, and, without knowing what she did, implored, with all the energy and expression of a mother in despair, for the life of her child. The noble animal stopped, fixed his glaring eye-balls upon her with a peculiar expression, regarded her for an instant, and immediately dropped the infant lightly on the ground, without having done him the smallest injury; then with a look of indescribable nobleness, quietly returned to his own habitation, and with the greatest docility suffered the keeper to replace him in his den.

Sucked To Death By A Bear

Captain Williamson says, it has often been in my way to see the operations of bears in India, and I am confident that no animals exist more cruel, more fierce, or more implacable than they are! Such as have suffered under their brutality, have, in all instances within my knowledge, borne the proofs of having undergone the most dilatory torments. Some have had their bones macerated with little breaking of the skin; others have had their flesh sucked away into long fibrous remnants, and in one instance the most horrid brutality was displayed.

While stationed at Dacca, I went with a party several times to the great house at Tergong, distant about five miles from the town. I had on several occasions seen bears among the wild mango topes, and did not consider them so dangerous, until one day, as I was returning with a friend from hunting some hog-deer, we heard a most lamentable outcry in the cover through which we had to pass.

Having our spears, and being provided with guns, we alighted, not doubting but a leopard had attacked some poor wood cutter. We met a woman whose fears had deprived her of speech, and whose senses were just flitting. She, however, recollected herself sufficiently to pronounce the word bauloo, which signifies a bear. She led us with caution, to a spot not more than fifty yards distant, where we found her husband extended on the ground, his hands and feet, as I before observed, sucked and chewed into a perfect pulp, the teguments of the limbs in general drawn from under the skin, and the skull mostly laid bare; the skin of it hanging down in long strips; obviously effected by their talons. What was most wonderful was, that the unhappy man retained his senses sufficiently to describe that he had been attacked by several bears, the woman said seven, one of which had embraced him while the others clawed him about the head, and bit at his arms and legs, seemingly in competition for the booty. We conveyed the wretched object to a house, where, in a few hours, death relieved him from a state, in which no human being could afford the smallest assistance!

Awful Somnolency

Samuel Clinton, a labouring man, about twenty-five years of age, on the 13th of May, 1694, fell into a profound sleep, out of which he could by no means be roused by those about him; but after a month's time he rose of himself, put on his clothes, and went about his business of a husbandman as usual. From this time to the month of April, 1696, he remained free from any extraordinary drowsiness, but then fell into his sleeping fit again. After some days his friends were prevailed on to try what remedies might effect, and accordingly one Mr Gibbs, an apothecary, bled, blistered, cupped, and scarified him, and used all the external irritating medicines he could think of, but all to no purpose. Victuals stood by him as before, which he ate now and then, but nobody ever saw him eat or evacuate, though he did both as he had occasion, and sometimes they found him fast asleep with the pot in his hand abed, and sometimes with his mouth full of meat. In this manner he lay till the 7th of August, which was seventeen weeks from the time he began to sleep, and then he awaked, put on his clothes, and walked about the room, not knowing he had slept so long, till going into the fields he found people busy in getting in their harvest, and he remembered that when he fell asleep, they were sowing the oats and barley. From this time he remained well till the 17th of August, 1697, when he complained of a shivering, and a coldness in his back, vomited once or twice, and the same day he fell asleep again. Dr Oliver (from whom this account is taken) went to see him, and felt his pulse, which was then very regular, he was in a breathing sweat, and had an agreeable warmth all over his body. The doctor then put his mouth to his ear, and called him as loud as he could several times, pulled him by the shoulders, pinched his nose, stopped his mouth and nostrils, but to no purpose; the man not giving the least sign of his being sensible.

Upon this the doctor held a phial with sal-almoniac under one of his nostrils, but it only made his nose run, and his eyelids shiver and tremble a little. Finding no success this way, the doctor crammed that nostril with powder of white hellebore, and waited some time to see what effect it would produce, but the man did not discover the least uneasiness. The doctor then left him, fully satisfied that he was really asleep, and no sullen counterfeit as some people supposed. About ten days after, an apothecary took fourteen ounces of blood from his arm, tied it up again and left him as he found him, without his making the least motion all the while. The latter end of September Dr Oliver saw him again, and a gentleman ran a large pin into his arm to the very bone, but he gave no signs of being sensible of what was done to him. In this manner he lay till the 19th of November, when his mother hearing him make a noise, ran immediately up to him, and found him eating: she asked him how he did; very well, he said, thank God – and again she asked him which he liked best, bread and butter, or bread and cheese; he answered bread and cheese. Whereupon the woman, overjoyed, ran down stairs to acquaint his brother of it, and both coming up again, they found him as fast asleep as ever. Thus he continued till the end of January or beginning of February, at which time he awakened perfectly well, remembering nothing that happened all the while. It was observed that he was very little altered in his flesh, only he complained the cold pinched him more than usual, and so went about his business as at other times.– This Clinton lived at Tensbury, near Bath.

Flying

Knolles, in his History of the Turks, gives the following relation of an attempt at flying, made at Constantinople about the year 1147, during the visit of Clisasthlan the Turkish sultan, to Emanuel the Greek emperor.

'Amongst the quaint devices of many for solemnizing so great a triumph, there was an active Turk, who had openly given it out, that against an appointed time, he would, from the top of a high tower in a tilt yard, fly the space of a furlong; the report whereof had filled the city with a wonderful expectation of so great a novelty. The time prefixed being come, and the people without number assembled, the Turk, according to his promise, upon the top of a high tower shewed himself, girt in a long large white garment, gathered into many plaits and foldings, made on purpose for the gathering of the wind; wherewith the foolish man had vainly persuaded himself to have hovered in the air, as do birds upon the wings, or to have guided himself, as are ships with their sails. Standing thus hovering a great while, as ready to take this flight, the beholders still laughing and crying out, 'Fly, Turk! fly! How long shall we expect thy flight?' The Emperor in the meantime still kept dissuading from so desperate an attempt; and the sultan, betwixt fear and hope, hanging in doubtful suspense what might happen to his country man. The Turk, after he had a great while hovered with his arms abroad (the better to have gathered the wind, as birds do with their wings), and long deluded the expectation of the beholders, at length finding the wind fit, as he thought, for this purpose, committed himself with his vain hope into the air; but instead of mounting aloft, this foolish Icarus came tumbling down with such violence, that he broke his neck, his arms, his legs, with almost all the bones of his body.'

Unfortunate Similarity Of Person

In the year 1727, Thomas Geddely lived as a waiter with Mrs Hannah Williams, who kept a public-house at York. It being a house of much business, and the mistress very assiduous therein, she was deemed in wealthy circumstances. One morning her scrutoire was found broken open and robbed, and Thomas Geddely disappearing at the same time, there was no doubt as to the robber. About a twelvemonth after, a man calling himself James Crow, came to York, and worked a few days for a precarious subsistence, by carrying goods as a porter. By this time he had been seen by many, who accosted him as Thomas Geddely.— He declared he did not know them, as his name was James Crow, and that he was never at York before. This was held as merely a trick, to save himself from the consequences of the robbery committed in the house of Mrs Williams, when he lived with her as a waiter.

He was apprehended, his mistress sent for; and, in the midst of many people, she instantly singled him out, called him by his name, (Thomas Geddely) and charged him with his unfaithfulness and ingratitude in robbing her.

He was directly taken before a justice of the peace; but, on his examination, absolutely affirmed that he was not Thomas Geddely, that he knew no such person, that he never was at York before, and that his name was James Crow. Not, however, giving good account of himself, but rather admitting himself to be a petty rogue and vagabond, and Mrs Williams and another swearing positively to his person, he was committed to York Castle for trial, at the next assizes.

On arraignment, he pleaded not guilty; still denying that he was the person he was taken for. But Mrs Williams and some others swearing that he was the identical Thomas Geddely who lived with her when she was robbed, and who went off immediately on the commitment of the robbery; and a servant girl deposed, she saw the prisoner that very morning in the room where the scrutoire was broken open, with a poker in his hand; and the prisoner being unable to prove an alibi, he was found guilty of the robbery. He was soon after executed, but persisted to his latest breath, that he was not Thomas Geddely, and that his name was James Crow.

And so it proved: for some time after the true Thomas Geddely, who, on robbing his mistress, had fled York to Ireland, was taken up in Dublin, for a crime of the same stamp, and there condemned and executed.– Between his conviction and execution, and again at the fatal tree, he confessed himself to be the very Thomas Geddely who had committed the robbery at York, for which the unfortunate James Crow had been executed.

We must add, that a gentleman, an inhabitant of York, happening to be in Dublin at the time of Geddely's execution, and who knew him when he lived with Mrs Williams, declared, that the resemblance between the two men was so exceedingly great, that it was next to impossible for the nicest eye to have distinguished their persons asunder.

Thunder-Storm in Norfolk

On the 20th July 1655, being the Sabbath day, about four of the clock in the afternoon, there was a great and sudden tempest in the city of Norwich, and the country thereabouts; the flashes of lightning were most dreadful and violent, and the loud claps from the clouds did so amaze and affright the people, that they thought the spheres came thundering down in flames about their ears. About an hour afterwards, there appeared to the view of many, a black cloud of smoke, like unto the smoke of a furnace, and ever and anon it did cast forth flames of fire; it was attended with a white cloud, which, sailing along the air, did seem to labour for all the advantages of the wind, to overtake the other; but, the black cloud being first come, and covering the face of the city, there arose a sudden whirlwind, which in the streets of the city did raise such a dust, that it was almost impossible for one man to discern any other, but only at a little distance; and, to increase this wonderful darkness, the clouds grew thicker and thicker, especially at the south and south-west, when behold the lightning from them did leap forth again, and the thunder child, and there followed such a rattling storm of stupendous hail, that being afterwards measured, the hail-stones were found to be five inches about, and some more; all the glass windows that were on the weather-side of the city were beaten down.

Some letters from Norwich do affirm, that three thousand pounds will not repair the windows. This which I now speak, may in other countries seem incredible, and so it might be in our own also, were it not attested by about ten thousand witnesses.– And surely it is well worth the observation of all the best philosophers to take notice, that those hail-stones (as they exceeded all others in their bigness, so they were unlike them in their form), for many of them were mere pieces of flat ice, and had not the least similitude of roundness in them. It is to be admired besides, that in many of these hail-stones, there was to be seen the figure of an eye, resembling the eye of a man, and that so perfectly, as if it had been there engraved by the hand of some skilful artificer.

If your eyes, possessed with these unusual spectacles, have yet the leisure to look into the country, in hope there to behold some more comfortable objects, you will find in some places whole fields of corn destroyed by lightning; you will behold the tempest wrestling with the trees, and having torn them up by the roots, to lay them on their backs with their heels higher than their heads; the burrows could not protect the listening conies, nor the trees the birds; but the next morning the travellers found them dead in great numbers on the ground, and in some places a horse or cow lying by them. The lightning whirled through the whole country, and passing through some houses where the windows were made one against the other, it was seen afterwards to run all along, and to lick the ground; many houses were fired by it, and had it not pleased God to send an extraordinary shower of rain, some towns that had taken fire had been undoubtedly destroyed. It struck some men and women dead for the present, whom it pleased God to recover again to life, to magnify his mercies, and to declare his wonders.

Ferocious Attack Of A Lioness Upon the Exeter Mail

The Exeter Mail Coach on its way to London was attacked on Sunday night, October 20th, 1816, at Wilmerslow-hut, seven miles from Salisbury, in a most extraordinary manner. At the moment when the coachman pulled up to deliver his bags, one of the leaders was suddenly seized by a ferocious animal; this produced great confusion and alarm; two passengers who were inside the mail got out, ran into the house, and locked themselves up in a room above stairs, the horses kicked and plunged violently, and it was with great difficulty the coachman could prevent the carriage from being overturned. It was soon perceived by the coachman and guard, by the light of the lamps, that the animal which had seized the horse was a huge lioness. A large mastiff dog came up and attacked her fiercely, on which she quitted the horse and turned upon him. The dog fled, but was pursued and killed by the lioness within about forty yards of the place. It appears that the beast had escaped from a caravan that was standing on the road side belonging to the proprietors of a menagerie, on their way to Salisbury fair. An alarm being given, the keepers pursued and hunted the lioness into a hovel under a granary. About half past eight they had secured her so effectually, by barricading the place, as to prevent her escape. The horse, when first attacked, fought with great spirit, and if at liberty would probably have beaten down his antagonist with his fore-feet, but in plunging he embarrassed himself in the harness. The lioness it appears had attacked him in the front, and springing at his throat, had fastened the talons of her fore-feet on each side of the neck close to the head, while the talons of her hind-feet were forced into the chest. In this situation she hung, while the blood was seen flying as if a vein had been opened by a lancet. The ferocious animal missed the throat and the jugular vein, but the horse was so dreadfully torn, as to leave no hopes of life; the expression of

agony in his tears and moans was most piteous and affecting. A fresh horse having been procured the mail drove on
after having been detained three quarters of an hour by this
extraordinary obstruction.

It was not ascertained when the mail-coach drove off from
Winterslow that the ferocious animal which made the attack
was actually secured. She seemed, however, not to be in any
immediate hurry to move, for whether she had carried off
with her, as prey, the dog she had killed, or from some other
cause, she continued growling and howling in so loud a tone
that they could hear her for nearly half a mile. Nothing could
exceed the anxiety of all present to have the animal killed,
and they called out loudly to the guard to dispatch it with
his blunderbuss, which he was disposed to do; but the owner
cried out to him, 'For God's sake don't kill her, she cost me
£500, and she will be as quiet as a lamb if not irritated.' This
arrested his hand, and he did not fire, although strongly urged
by the passengers.

The lioness was a very fine animal, then only five years old; and the manner in which she was secured after her attack on the horse affords a proof of the extreme state of tameness to which such creatures are brought by the management of their keepers. When she had retired under the granary, her owner and assistant followed her upon their hands and knees with lighted candles, and having placed a sack on the ground near her, they made her lie down upon it, then tied her four legs and passed a cord round her mouth which they secured, in this state they drew her out upon the sack and she was then carried by six men into her den in the caravan. To the astonishment of every one who beheld this part of the transaction, which lasted about a quarter of an hour, the lioness lay as quiet as a lamb during her removal to the caravan; but when she was there she became sensible of the restraint and her rage was excessive till the cords were loosed.

Nobility Of Blood

Crantz, in his Saxon History, tells us of an Earl of Alsatia, surnamed, on account of his great strength, Iron; who was a great favourite with Edward the Third of England, and much envied, as favourites are always sure to be, by the rest of the courtiers. On one occasion, when the king was absent, some noblemen maliciously instigated the queen to make a trial of the noble blood of the favourite, by causing a lion to be let loose upon him, saying, 'according to the popular belief, that 'if the earl was truly noble the lion would not touch him.' It being customary with the earl to rise at the break of day, before any other person in the palace was stirring, a lion was let loose during the night, and turned into the lower court. When the earl came down in the morning, with no more than a night-gown cast over his shirt, he was met by the lion bristling his hair, and growling destruction between his teeth. The earl not in the least daunted, called out with a stout voice, 'Stand, you dog!' At these words the lion couched at his feet, to the great amazement of the courtiers, who were peeping out at every window, to see the issue of their ungenerous object. The earl laid hold of the lion by the mane, turned him into his cage, and placing his nightcap on the lion's back, came forth without ever casting a look behind him. 'Now,' said the earl, calling out to the courtiers, whose presence at the windows instantly convinced him of the share they had had in this trial of his courage, 'Let him amongst you all, that standeth most upon his pedigree, go and fetch my night-cap.'

A Remarkable Instance Of Courage In A French Officer

During the war of 1759, Count de B., a young nobleman, not twenty years of age, going on horseback from a town in Burgundy to join his regiment, was attacked by a mad wolf of an extraordinary size. The furious animal first seized the horse, and tore off such large pieces of flesh, that M. de B. was soon dismounted. Then the wolf flew at him, and would certainly have tore him to pieces, had he not great presence of mind. With one hand he seized the wolf's foaming tongue, and with the other laid hold of his paws; after struggling awhile with the terrible creature, the tongue slipt from him, and his right thumb was bitten off; upon which, notwithstanding the pain he was in, he leaped upon the wolf's back, clapt his knees fast to his flanks, and called for help to some armed peasants who were passing by, but none of these fellows dared advance; 'Well then, says he, 'fire, if you kill me, I forgive you.' One of them fired, and three bullets went through the brave officer's coat, but neither he nor the beast were wounded. Another, bolder than his comrades, seeing the cavalier was intrepid, and kept firm upon the wolf, came very near, and let fly at him; the animal was mortally wounded by this shot, and, after a few more furious motions, expired. In this dreadful conflict, besides the losing of his right thumb, the young count's left arm was torn, and he got several bites on his legs and thighs.

Preservation Of Human Bodies After Their Decease

An intelligent tourist who visited the city of Bremen, in Germany, in 1774, says there is one peculiarity belonging to this city, of the reality of which nothing but occular demonstration could have convinced me. Under the Cathedral church, is a vaulted apartment, supported on pillars; it is near sixty paces long, and half as many broad. The light and the air are constantly admitted into it by three windows, though it is several feet below the level of the ground. Here are five large oak coffers, each containing a corpse, which without being embalmed, have suffered no corruption. I examined them severally for near two hours. The most curious and perfect, is that of a woman. Tradition says, she was an English countess, who dying at Bremen about two hundred and fifty years ago, ordered her body to be placed in this vault uninterred, in the apprehension that her relations would cause it to be brought over to her native country. Though the muscular skin is totally dried in every part, yet so little are the features of the face or skin changed, that nothing is more certain than she was young, and even beautiful. It is a small countenance, sound in its contour; the cartilage of the nose and nostrils have undergone no laceration: her teeth are all firm in the sockets, but the lips are drawn away from over them. The cheeks are sunk in, yet less than I ever remember to have seen in embalmed bodies. The hair of her head is more than eighteen inches long, and very thick, and so fast, that I heaved the corpse out of the coffin by it: the colour is light brown, and as fresh and glossy as that of a living person. That this lady was of high rank seems evident from the extreme fineness of the linen which covers her body; but I in vain endeavoured to procure any light into her history, her title, or any particulars, though I took no little pains for that purpose. The landlord in the inn, who served as my conductor, said he remembered it for forty years past, during which time there is not the least perceptible alteration in it. In another coffer is the body of a workman, who is said to have tumbled off the church, and was killed by the fall. His features evince this most forcibly. Extreme agony is marked in them; his mouth is wide open, and his eye-lids the same; the eyes are dried up. His breast is unnaturally distended, and his whole frame betrays a violent death.–A little child who died of the small-pox, is still more remarkable. The marks of the pustules, which have broken the skin on his hands and head, are very discernible; and one would suppose, that a body, which died of such a distemper, must contain, in a high degree, the seeds of putrefaction.– The other corpses are likewise very extraordinary.

There are in this vault, likewise, turkeys, hawks, weasels, and other animals, which have been hung up here, from time immemorial, some very lately, and are all in the most complete preservation, and unaltered in their parts. The cause of this phenomenon is doubtless the dryness of the place where they are laid. It is in vain to seek for any other. The magistrates do not permit any fresh bodies to be brought here, and there is no subterranean chamber which has the same property. It would have made an excellent miracle two or three centuries ago in proper hands; but now mankind are grown too wise.

The Maid And The Magpie

A noble lady of Florence lost a valuable pearl necklace, and one of her waiting-women (a very young girl) was accused of the theft. Having solemnly denied the fact, she was put to the torture, which was given à plaisir at Florence. Unable to support its terrible infliction, she acknowledged that 'she was guilty', and without further trial, was hung. Shortly after, Florence was visited by a tremendous storm; a thunderbolt fell on the figure of Justice, and split the scales, one of which fell to the earth, and with it fell the ruins of a magpie's nest, containing the pearl necklace! Those scales are still the haunt of birds.

A Human Body Found In A Bear Skin

A dead body was landed at Cadiz, enclosed in a long skin nearly resembling that of a bear; it was found, with several others of the same kind, in some caverns in the Canary Islands, where they are supposed to have been buried before the conquest of those islands by John de Bretancourt, a Norman, in 1417, or by Peter de Vera, a Spaniard, in 1433. The flesh of this body is perfectly preserved, but is dry, inflexible, and hard as wood, so that to the touch it seems petrified, though it is not. The features of the face are very perfect, and appear to be those of a young man; nor is that, or any other part of the body, decayed. The body is no more shrunk than if the person had not been dead above two or three days. The skin only, appears a little shrivelled, this body was sent to Madrid, to be deposited in the royal academy of surgery. The case, in which it was placed, had another small case within it, containing two or three vases, and a hand-mill, which were found in the same cavern.

&

An Archbishop Devoured By Rats

In the middle of the river Rhine, in Germany, is a strong tower, built on a small island, called Mauss Thurn, i.e. the Tower of Rats, which devoured the barbarous archbishop Hatton.

The tradition is, that Hatton, the second archbishop of Mayence, surnamed Bonose, Duke of Franconia, and Abbot of Fulden, who, under the fairest outside, covered the heart of a Nero, governed, during the first year of his prelateship, with great mildness; but in the second, a terrible famine having happened in that country, finding himself daily tormented by a vast number of people who came to beg their bread of him, he gathered them together in a barn, under the pretence of ordering corn to be distributed among them: these poor souls no sooner entered it, in hopes to get the corn that had been promised them, than the inhuman prelate ordered the doors to be barricaded, and fire to be set to the place; and thus put to death, in the cruellest manner, about five hundred persons, among whom were a great number of women and infants.

He even had the barbarity to say, that these vermin were a kind of rats, which were good for nothing but to consume the fruits of the earth, and consequently prejudicial to the public.

Soon after a multitude of rats assembling from all quarters, rushed upon the archbishop, and pursued him, wherever he fled to shelter himself from them.

This inhuman miscreant thought he could escape the divine vengeance by retiring into a tower, standing in the middle of the river Rhine; but these animals swam after him, and in spite of all his efforts to hinder them, fell upon and devoured this detestable prelate; and it is said that they even ate his name in the church and other public places, where it had been affixed up.

The Tarantula

The tarantula, a venomous kind of spider, is found chiefly in Naples, near the city of Taranto, from whence the insect derives its name. The tarantula is about the size of a large nutmeg, furnished with eight legs, and as many eyes; it is hairy, and of various colours. From its mouth arise two horns, or trunks, formed a little crooked, with the points exceedingly sharp, though which it conveys its poison. These horns are in continual motion, especially when the animal is seeking for food; whence it is conjectured, that they are a kind of moveable nostrils. Tarantulas are also found in various parts of Italy; but those of Apulia, in which the city of Taranto stands, are the only kind that are reckoned dangerous, and that chiefly in the heat of summer. The bite or sting of this insect occasions a pain like that felt on the stinging of a bee or ant; and in a few hours a livid circle appears about the part affected, which is followed by a painful swelling. Soon after this the afflicted person falls into a profound sadness, breathes with difficulty, and at length loses all sense and motion. Some people who are wounded express great satisfaction at the sight of particular colours, and a strange aversion to others. Tremblings, anger, fear, laughter, weeping, absence, talk, and action, are also symptoms attending persons bit by the tarantula, who infallibly die in a few days, unless proper means are used to expel the poison. All the assistance that medicine has yet discovered consists in some external applications on the wound, in cordials and sudorifics. But these are of little efficacy, music being the only remedy. As soon as the patient has lost his sense and motion, a musician is sent for, who tries several tunes on an instrument, till he hits on that which is most agreeable to the disordered person. This is known by his first moving his fingers, then his arms, afterwards his legs, and by degrees his whole body, till at length he rises on his feet, and begins to dance, which he continues for several hours. After this he is put to bed, and when he is judged to have sufficiently recruited his strength, the musician calls him out of bed by the same tune, to take a second dance. This exercise is repeated for four or five days, till the patient grows weary and unable to dance any longer, which is a sign of his being cured. When he comes to himself, he is like one awaked out of a profound sleep, not having the least recollection of the dancing, or of any thing that passed during the time of his disorder. If the cure be not completely effected, the patient continues melancholy, shuns company, and perhaps drowns himself, if he has an opportunity. Some have had regular returns of their fits, every twelve months, for a great many years successively, at which times they are treated in the manner already described, finding no relief from any thing but music and dancing.

Dr Mead, in his curious treatise on the effect of the bite of the tarantula, supposes that the malignity of this poison to consist in its great force and energy, whereby it immediately raises an extraordinary fermentation in the whole arterial fluid. As to the tarantula, (those bit by the tarantula) he says, the benefit of music arises, not from their dancing to it, and so evacuating sweat, a great part of the poison; but the percussions and vibrations of the air break the cohesion of the parts of the blood, and prevent coagulation; so that the heat being removed by sweating, and the coagulation by the contraction of the muscular fibrillae, the wounded person is restored to his former condition.

The Botocudos Of Brazil

Prince Maximilian of Wied-Nenwied, when travelling in Brazil, witnessed a singular battle fought by two tribes of the Botocudos. The cause of their quarrel was, that Captain June, with his people, had been hunting on the south bank of the river St Matthew, on the grounds of Captain Japarack, and killed some swine. This was considered by the latter as a great insult, only to be atoned for by war.

First, the warriors of both parties uttered short rough tones of defiance to each other, walking sullenly round each other like angry dogs, and at the same time making ready their poles. Captain Japarack then came forward, walked about between the men, looked gloomily and directly before him with wide staring eyes, and sung, with a tremulous voice, a long song, which he had received. In this manner the adverse parties became more and more inflamed; suddenly two of them advanced, and pushed one another with the arms on the breast, so that they staggered back, and then began to ply their poles. One first struck with all his might at the other regardless of where the blow fell; his antagonist bore the first attack seriously and calmly, without changing countenance; he then took his turn, and thus they belaboured each other with severe blows, the marks of which long remained visible on their naked bodies. As there were left on the poles many sharp stumps of branches which had been cut off, the effect of the blows was not always confined to bruises, but the blood flowed from the heads of many of the combatants. When two of them had thus thrashed each other handsomely, two more came forward; and several pairs were often seen engaged at once; but they never laid hands on one another. When these combats had continued for some time, they again walked about with a serious look, uttering tones of defiance, till heroic enthusiasm again seized them, and set their poles in motion.

Meanwhile, the woman also fought valiantly; amidst continual weeping and howling, they seized each other by the hair, struck with their fists, scratched with their nails, tore the plugs of wood (which the Botocudos wear) out of each other's ears and lips, and scattered them on the field of battle as trophies. If one threw her adversary down, a third, who stood behind, seized her by the legs, and threw her down likewise, and then they pulled each other about on the ground. The men did not degrade themselves so far as to strike the women of the opposite party, but only pushed them with the end of their poles, or kicked them on the side, so that they rolled over and over. The lamentations and howlings of the women, and the children likewise, resounded from the neighbouring huts, and heightened the effect of this most singular scene.

In this manner the combat continued for about an hour, when all appeared weary; some of the savages showed their courage and perseverance, by walking about among the others, uttering their tones of defiance. Captain Japarack, as the principal person of the offended party, held out to the last; all seemed fatigued and exhausted, when he, not yet disposed to make peace, continued to sing his tremulous song, and encouraged his people to renew combat, till prince Maximilian went up to him, and told him that he was a valiant warrior, but that it was now time to make peace; upon which, he at length suddenly quitted the field, and went over to the Quartel. Captain June had not shown so much energy; being an old man, he had taken no part in the combat, but constantly remained in the background.

Awful Visitation

A gentleman in Virginia, being one day standing at his window, and smoking his pipe, looking on the country, it being a very calm fine day, on a sudden, a violent clap of thunder bursted near him, and struck him dead; and what was very remarkable, was, that he immediately became stiff, so that he did not fall, but remained, leaning in the window, with his pipe in his mouth, and in the same posture he was in when he received the stroke, by which means it was some time before it was discovered that he was dead, as the thunder did no damage to the room or window where he was.

A Child Born With Three Eyes

At Arlington, in the county of Durham, in the year 1609, Mary Travers, the wide of Thomas Travers, plumber and glazier, was delivered of a female child, who had three eyes; two of which were in the common part of the face, and the third was placed directly above the nose, in the middle of the forehead; and what adds to the wonder of this phenomenon is, that the right eye was of a fine hazel colour, the left was blue, and the eye in the middle of the forehead was grey. The child died about two hours after its birth.

The truth of this affair was attested by the midwife, a physician, surgeon, and six of the neighbours of good credit.

There is now in the British Museum, a child with three eyes, preserved in spirits, which was a part of the late Sir Hans Sloane's collection of curiosities.

God's Judgement On A Bishop

John Cameron, bishop of Glasgow in Scotland, was so given to covetousness, extortion, violence, and oppression, especially upon his own tenants and vassals, he would scarcely afford them bread to eat or clothes to cover their nakedness. But the night before Christmas-day, and in the middle of all his cruelties, as he lay in bed at his house in Lockwood, he heard a voice, summoning him to appear before the tribunal of Christ, and give an account of his actions. Being terrified with this notice, and the pangs of a guilty conscience, he called up his servants, commanding them to bring lights and stay in the room with him.

He himself took a book in his hand, and began to read, but the voice being a second time heard, struck all the servants with horror. The same voice repeating the summons a third time, and with a louder and more dreadful accent, the bishop, after a lamentable and frightful groan, was found dead in his bed, with his tongue hanging out of his mouth, a dreadful spectacle to all beholders. This relation is made by the celebrated Buchanan, who records it as a remarkable example of God's judgement against the sin of oppression.

Remarkable Earthquake

In 1692 an earthquake happened at Jamaica, attended with almost all the terrible circumstances imaginable. In two minutes it destroyed the town of Port-Royal, at that time the capital of the island; and sunk the houses in a gulph forty fathoms deep. It was attended with a hollow noise like that of thunder; the streets rose like the waves of the sea, first lifting up the houses, and then immediately throwing them down into deep pits. All the wells discharged their waters with the most violent agitation. The sea burst over its bounds. The fissures of the earth were in some places so great, that one of the streets appeared twice as broad as formerly. In many places it opened and closed again; and continued this agitation for some time. Of these openings great numbers might be seen at a time. In some of them the people were swallowed up at once; in others, the earth caught them by the middle, and crushed them to death; while others, more fortunate, were swallowed up in one chasm, and thrown out alive by another. Some chasms were large enough to swallow up whole streets; and others, still more formidable, spouted up immense quantities of water, drowning such as the earthquake had spared. The whole was attended with stenches and offensive smells, the noise of falling mountains at a distance, &c. and the sky, in a minute's time, turned dull and red, like a glowing oven.

Yet, as great a sufferer as Port-Royal was, more houses were left standing therein than on the whole island besides. Scarce a planting-house, or sugar-house, was left standing in all Jamaica. A great part of them were swallowed up, houses, people, trees, and all in one gap; instead of which afterwards appeared great pools of water; which, when dried up, left nothing but sand, without any mark that ever tree or plant had grown thereon. The shock was so violent, that it threw people on their knees or their faces, as they were running about for shelter. Several houses were shuffled some yards out of their places, and yet continued standing. One Hopkins had his plantation removed half a mile from where it stood, without any considerable alteration. All the wells in the island, as well as those of Port-Royal, from one fathom to six or seven deep, threw their water out at the top with great violence. About twelve miles from the sea, the earth gaped, and spouted out, with a prodigious force, vast quantities of water into the air; yet the greatest violence was among the rocks and mountains; and it is the general opinion, that the nearer the mountains, the greater the shock; and that the cause thereof lay among them. Most of the rivers were stopped up for twenty-four hours by the falling of the mountains; till, welling up, they made themselves new tracks and channels; tearing up, in their passage, trees, &c.

After the great shock, those people who escaped got on board the ships in the harbour, where they continued about two months; the shocks all that time being so violent, and coming so thick, sometimes two or three in an hour, accompanied with frightful noises like a rushing wind, or a hollow rumbling thunder, with brimstone blasts, that they durst not come on shore. The consequence of the earthquake was a general sickness, from the noisesome vapours belched forth, which swept away about three thousand persons.

Fearful Encounter With A Tiger

Colonel Duff was perhaps one of the strangest and coolest men in the moment of enterprise and danger of any man in Europe. One day, he went from the settlement where he was stationed, in company with two of his most intimate friends on a shooting party. After having explored various coverts which promised game, they were unexpectedly surprised by the spring of a tyger. The colonel instantly levelled his piece and wounded him. The tyger instantly sprang on him, striking his talons into his cheek and neck, the flesh of which he tore away as effectually as if it had been done by a cannon ball. In the attempts to parry him, the barrel of his fowling piece was bent double. The colonel, in the shock of this attack, fell against the stump of a tree, which put him in that precise posture wherein he could best exert his strength. He grappled his antagonist by the throat, and setting his knee against the chest of this fierce animal, threw him fairly from him. The tyger, astonished at so uncommon a reception, turned tail, and absolutely ran off. His friends, at the moment of his recontre, had fled with the utmost precipitation, and had returned to the settlement to relate the sad story of the colonel's fate. As the action was short, the colonel was not long after them, and personally contradicted the report of the enemy having carried him by storm, though he acknowledged that his outworks had received some injury.

A Man And Child Burnt To Death By Lightning

In the reign of king James, in the year 1613, on the 26th of June, in the parish of Christ-church, Hampshire, one John Hithel, a carpenter, lying in bed with a young child was, together with the child, burnt to death by a sudden flash of lightning; no fire appeared outwardly upon them, and yet they lay burning for the space of almost three days, till they were quite consumed to ashes.

Prematurity

On the 14th of March, 1729, was born Charles, the son of Richard Charlesworth, a carrier, at Longnor, in the county of Stafford. At his birth he was under the common size, but he grew so amazingly fast, that before he was four years old, he was nearly four feet high, and in strength, agility, and bulk, equal to a fine boy of ten years old. At five he was four feet seven inches high, weighed eighty-seven pounds, and could with ease carry a man of fourteen stone weight, had hair on his body as a man, and every sign of puberty, and worked as a man at his father's business; this was the time of his full vigour, from whence he began to decrease in strength and bulk, like a man in the decline of life; and at the age of seven years his strength was gone, his body was totally emaciated, his eyes were sunk, his head was palsical, and he died with all the signs of extreme old age, as if the months he had lived had been years.

Fire-Eaters

Rodericus Fonseca, a physician of great reputation at Pisa, bought for his household employment, a slave, which as often as she pleased took burning coals into her hand or mouth without any hurt at all. This was confirmed to me (says the author) by Gabriel Fonseca, a celebrated physician in Rome; who told me he had frequently seen the trial, and red hot coals held in her hand until they were almost cold, and this without any impression left upon her: and I myself saw the same thing done by a female, in the hospital of the Holy Ghost, of which I was a physician.

It is familiarly known all over Pisa, of Martinus Ceccho, a townsman of Montelupo, that he used to take hot coals in his hand, put them into his mouth, and bite them into pieces with his teeth till he had extinguished them. He would tread upon them with his bare feet. He would put boiling lead into his mouth, and suffer a burning candle to be held under his tongue, as he put it out of his mouth; and many other such things as may seem incredible; all this was confirmed to me by divers Capuchins, and my worthy friend Nicholas Accunsius, of the order of St Francis.

A Child Nurtured By A Wolf

Some gentleman hunting in the forest of Arden, in Picardy, slew a she-wolf, that was followed by a child of about seven years of age, stark naked, of a strange complexion, and with fair curled hair. The child seeing the wolf dead, ran fiercely at them, was beset and taken. The nails of his hands and feet bowed inward: he spake nothing, but uttered only inarticulate sounds. Having brought him to a neighbouring town, they manacled his hands and feet; and, by long fasting, brought him to tameness, so that in seven months he was taught to speak.

By circumstances of time, and six fingers he had on one hand, he was found to be the child of a woman, who stealing wood, was pursued by officers, and in her fright left her child, then about nine months old, which, as is supposed, was carried away by the she-wolf, and by her nurtured to the time of his being taken.

He afterwards became a herdsman, for seven years, during which time, wolves never made an attempt upon his flock, though they were very numerous. This being observed by the neighbouring villages, many people committed their cattle to his care; by which means he acquired great store of money, and lived and died in comfort and affluence.

Isaaco And The Crocodile

Mr Park's guide, Isaaco, as the party were passing one of the rivers, was very active in pushing the asses into the water, and shoving along the canoe; but being afraid that they would not all be got over in the course of the day, he attempted to drive six of the asses across the river a little farther down, where the water was shallower. When he reached the middle of the river, a crocodile rose close to him, and instantly seizing him by the left thigh, pulled him under the water. With wonderful presence of mind he felt for the head of the animal, and thrust his finger into its eye; on which it quitted its hold, and Isaaco attempted to reach the further shore, calling out for a knife. But the crocodile returned, and seized him by the other thigh, and again pulled him under water; he had recourse to the same expedient, and thrust his fingers into its eyes with such violence, that it again quitted him; and when it rose, it flounced about on the surface of the water as if stupid, and then swam down the middle of the river. Isaaco proceeded to the other side, bleeding very much: as soon as the canoe returned, Mr Park went over, and found him much lacerated; but through the surgical assistance he was able to afford him, his wounds were gradually healed.

A Singular Instance Of Cornutation

Mr George Ash, secretary of the Dublin society, in a letter to one of the secretaries of the Royal Society, relates the story of a girl named Anne Jackson, born of English parents in the city of Waterford in Ireland, from whose body, when about three years old, horns grew out of several places, wherefore the mother concealed her out of shame, and bred her up privately; but she soon after dying, and her father being poor, she was thrown on the parish. When she was between thirteen and fourteen years old, she could scarcely go alone, and was no taller than a child of five years old; she was very silly, spoke but little, and that not plainly; her voice was low and rough, her complexion and face well enough, except her eyes, which were dead; and she could hardly perceive the difference of colours. The horns abounded chiefly about the joints and textures, and were fastened to the skin like warts; and about the roots resembled them much in substances, though towards the extremities they grew much harder and more horny. At the end of each finger and toe grew a horn as long as the finger or toe, not straight, but bending like a turkey's claw. On the other joints of her fingers or toes were smaller horns, which sometimes fell off, and others grew in their places. On her knees and elbows, and round about joints were many horns; two more remarkable at the point of each elbow, which twisted like ram's horns; that on the left arm was above an inch broad, and four inches long. At her armpits and the nipples of her breasts, small hard substances shot out, much whiter and more slender than the rest. At each ear also grew a horn; and the skin of her neck was callous and horny, like that of her hands and feet. She ate and drank heartily, slept soundly, and performed all the offices of nature like other healthy people.

A Worm Found In The Heart Of A Horse

On the seventeenth of March, 1586, Mr Dorrington of Spaldwick in the county of Huntingdon, one of the gentlemen pensioners to queen Elizabeth, had a horse, that died suddenly, which being opened, there was found in the hole of the heart, a strange kind of worm, that lay in a round head, in a caul or skin, of a likeness of a toad, which being taken out and spread, was in shape not to be described: it was divided into many grains, to the number of fifty, spread from the body like the branches of a tree; its length, from the snout to the end of the longest grain, seventeen inches, having four issues from which there dropped a red water: the body was of the colour of a mackerel, and three inches and a half round. It tried to crawl away, but was stabbed with a dagger, and its skin being stuffed, was shewn to queen Elizabeth, and most of the principal nobility of the kingdom.

Pyramid Of Human Heads

'I was shewn,' says Baron de Tott, 'on my journey to Jaff, as I approached the coast, the horrible pyramid erected by

Mehemet Bey. That barbarian Dgezar had formed it of fifteen hundred human heads, which he had caused to be cut off after taking the city.'

A Remarkable Disease In The Bones

Mr Henry Thompson, surgeon, communicates the following:–

James Stephenson, a shoemaker, in Wapping, aged thirty-three, five feet seven inches high, enjoyed a good state of health till about the year 1766, when he was seized with violent pains in his knees and feet, and was tormented with a head-ache, which came on at irregular periods; these pains he supposed to be rheumatic, and had recourse to a variety of medicines, and to empirical aid, without finding any alleviation whatever of his complaints. In the month of November, of the same year, he injured his left shoulder by a fall, which occasioned considerable pain and he was unable to move it for several months afterwards.

In November, 1768, he slipped down in his shop, and fancied he had sprained his right thigh; this confined him to his bed about a week: and he was afterwards unable to walk without the support of a person's arm and a crutch stick. On the twenty-first of December following, as he was endeavouring to go up stairs to bed, supported by his wife, he struck the toe of his right foot upon the edge of the step, and instantly cried out that his thigh was broken. He was put to bed, and an apothecary being sent for the next morning, who paying little attention to the injured thigh, attributed the great pain he suffered to an increase of his rheumatic complaints, and gave him medicines accordingly. In this situation he continued upwards of a fortnight, when Dr Dickson, physician to the London Hospital, was called in. Upon his viewing the thigh so much complained of, he found it crooked, and much shorter than the other, and therefore advised a surgeon to be sent for.

I saw him the following day, and on examination, found a fracture of the thigh bone near its upper extremity. I effected the reduction as well as I could, by means of very little extension; and had reason to suppose that the ends of the bone were in due contact, by the limb being equal length with the other. It was secured in this position by the usual apparatus; and I was in hopes that his pain would now cease: the event, however, proved different; his pain continued, though not so violent. This circumstance obliged me frequently to unbind the splints and to re-accommodate the bandage, judging that either the puckering of the bandage, or the tightness of the splints, might occasion in some measure the uneasiness which he felt. About the end of five weeks from the time I had replaced the thigh bone, desirous of knowing how far the union was completed, I undid the whole apparatus, and requested his wife lift up the leg, by placing one hand under the ham, and the other to embrace the leg above the ancle, whilst I examined the degree of firmness where the fracture had been. In doing this, I was surprised to find the thigh bone yield and fall in, about a hand's breath above the knee, similar to that of a fracture, excepting that in this case, there was no sensation of grating, as is usual where the broken bone is of a solid texture. Upon turning my head about to give his wife directions to lower the leg upon the pillow, I became more astonished, for I found the leg almost doubled in her hands; a similar separation of the two bones of the leg had taken place about a hand's breath below the tuberosity, as has been just before noticed, in the thigh bone. Both these separations were unaccompanied with any remarkable signs of additional pain to the patient.

This deplorable situation urged me to a particular inquiry into the case of so uncommon a calamity. I could however learn nothing satisfactory, further than concerning the rheumatic complaints before mentioned, which gave me some suspicion that a venereal virus might possibly have laid the foundation of the sufferings he had undergone, I questioned him upon this head: he acknowledged that he had a venereal complaint between two and three years before he married; that he never thought himself cured of it, though he had been married about six years; that he had scorbutic blotches upon him for some years, and declared he had then a gleet.

Upon viewing the eruption, I was confirmed in my opinion that it was venereal; I therefore resolved that he should begin a mercurial course, and accordingly directed a drachm of the strong mercurial ointment to be rubbed in every night, under the ham of the sound limb.

Previous to my dressing the miserable leg and thigh, I examined the separation, (for I could not call it fracture) which had been produced in the great bone of the leg. The skin being very thin, from the emaciated condition of the patient, I could perceive by the finger a regular transverse cleft in it: there was no appearance of ecchymosis nor tumefaction, nor did any appear afterwards: upon trying the surface of the bone with my fingers below the fissure, I found a remarkable softness and yielding of the bone down to its lower extremity, similar to a fluid contained therein. So extraordinary a circumstance excited my curiosity, and I determined to explore the nature of so uncommon a feel by laying it open. The following day I made an incision, about five inches in length, with a scalpel, through the skin, along the spine of the bone, and, turning the knife about an inch across upon the surface of the bone, I made a second incision parallel with the first, and then removed this incised portion clean from the periosteum, or skin which covers the bone, which was remarkably thin. Finding upon examination by my fingers, that the external part of the bone was extremely pliant and yielding, I passed my knife through it, and removed all that had been denuded with the greatest ease, its texture being only about the solidity and thickness of the rind of cheese.

This being done, I found a dusky red, or liver coloured flesh, occupying the whole internal part of the bone, devoid of sensibility, and from which the osseus covering had been removed, without the least haemorrhage: in short, it appeared to me an unorganised mass, similar to the flesh-like substance or coagulum which may be formed upon a stick or feather, by stirring fresh drawn blood in a basin.

The mercurial unction was continued every night for the space of a fortnight: the ptyalism gradually advanced, and he spat about a pint in the twenty-four hours when it arrived at its height. The wound on the leg suppurated in the most kindly manner, and healed in a short time. The spitting alleviated the pains in his limbs, the eruption upon the skin gradually disappeared, and, upon the whole, his health seemed much amended.

The right leg and thigh began to shorten, and acquired soon a considerable degree of deformity. The bandage and splints were discontinued, as being no longer serviceable; and, finding the bone of the left leg become softened in the manner which had been observed in that of the right, I lamented his fate, as judging him past all hope of relief.–However, his case being made known to the Medical Society, who from time to time assisted him with money, several of its members visited and directed the use of the various things. He drank wort for a considerable time, and likewise the antiscorbutic juices, and for a great while took a decoction of the bark with elixir of vitriol, by the order of Dr Dickson, who frequently saw him: but, nothing which was tried having any effect in checking the progress of the deplorable disease, the poor man grew tired of medicines, and calmly expected his dissolution.

From the time of my first attendance upon him to the day of his death, he was never able to be removed out of his bed; he lay upon his back, nor could he ever bear to be turned upon his side.

The left leg and thigh lost its straightness, and became deformed in like manner with the right; and, in proportion as the contraction and deformity took place, he gradually lost all sense of muscular action; but, when it became necessary to smooth the sheet under him, he was very sensible of pain, upon lifting up and laying down the limbs.

He was afterwards seized with a lientery, which put an end to a miserable existence on the 18th of February 1775, after a confinement to his bed of above six years.

Dr Hunter did me the favour of assisting in the examination of the body. Upon opening the chest, we found the ribs and breast bone had lost all their solidity, being easily cut through with a common scalpel; the cartilages of the ribs were unaltered; the contents of the chest and belly appeared in a healthy state, and were no otherwise affected than by situation, owing to the deformity of what originally formed the bony supports of the chest, the spine, and the hips. The gall bladder, however, was destitute of bile, greatly contracted, and contained a number of very small, black, jagged stones, resembling coal dust. We next proceeded to examine the state of every bone in the body; the result was, that we could easily pass the knife through those of the head, breast, ribs, vertebrae of the back and hips.

I have only to add, that the muscular parts in general, but more particularly of the lower extremities, were exceedingly pale, having lost the appearance of flesh, and it would scarcely have been possible to have traced them by dissection, from their contortion and adhesion to each other.

Curious Phenomenon

Dr James St John states that he has sometimes observed a phenomenon to take place during the putrefaction of human bodies, and which I cannot but think of great importance to be inquired into and known. This is the exhalation of a particular gas, which is the most active and dreadful of all corrosive poisons, and produces most sudden and terrible effects upon a living creature. This I have more than once had an opportunity of remarking in the dissecting-room of M. Andravi, at Paris; it not only is incapable of sustaining life in the absence of vital air, but it is dreadfully deleterious, and does not at all seem to abate of its corrosive property, even in the presence of the atmosphorical fluid. So that it is utterly dangerous to approach a body in this state of putrefaction. I have known a gentleman, who by slightly touching the intestine of a human body, beginning to liberate the corrosive gas, was affected with a violent inflammation, which, in a very short space of time, extended up almost the entire of his arm, producing an extensive ulcer for several months, and reduced him to a miserable state of emaciation. He then went to the south of France, but whether he died, or escaped with the loss of his arm, I have not been able to learn. I have known a celebrated professor, who was attached with a violent inflammation, from which he with difficulty recovered, by stooping for an instant over a body, which was beginning to give forth this deleterious fluid.

Terrific Conflict With A Rattle Snake

The ship Prosperity, from London, reached one of the West India islands in May, 1806. One of the seamen, named Jervas, having left the vessel, wandered about the island on a sultry day, such as are frequent in that part of the globe. Being oppressed by the intense heat, and fatigued with previous exertions, he inconsiderately laid himself down to sleep, relining his head on a small hillock, opposite a rock about ten feet high. He lay on his back, and his eyes, after he had slept a little, were directed, as the first object that met them, to the perpendicular height before him. What was his horror to discover, on top of it, an enormous rattle-snake with part of its body coiled up, and the other projecting considerably over the precipice, with its keen and beautiful, yet malignant eyes, steadily fixed on him! He felt as if charmed to the spot. The witchery of the serpent's eyes so irresistibly rooted him to the ground, that, for a moment, he did not WISH to remove from his formidable opponent. The huge reptile gradually and slowly uncoiled its body, all the while steadily keeping its eyes fixed on those of its intended victim.

Jervas now cried out, without being able to move, 'He'll bite me! take him away! take him away!'

The snake now began to writhe its body down a fissure in the rock, keeping its head elevated more than a foot from the ground. Its rattle made very little noise. It every moment darted out its forked tongue, its eyes became reddish and inflamed, and it moved rather quicker than at first. It was now within two yards of its intended victims, who by some means had dissipated the charm, and, roused by a sense of his awful danger, determined to stand on the defensive. To run away from it, he knew would be impracticable, as the snake would instantly dart its whole body after him. He therefore resolutely stood up, and put a strong glove on his right arm, which he happened to have with him. He stretched out his arm; the snake approached slowly and cautiously towards him, darting out its tongue still more frequently. Jervas recommended himself fervently to the protection of Heaven. The snake, when about a yard distant, made a violent spring. Jervas caught it in his right hand, directly under its head, and squeezed it with all his power. Its eyes almost started out of its head; it lashed its body on the ground, at the same time rattling loudly. He watched for an opportunity, and suddenly holding the animal's head, while for a moment it drew in its forked tongue, with his left hand, he, by a violent contraction of all the muscle in his hand, contrived to close effectually its jaws!

Much was NOW done, but much more was TO BE done. He had avoided much danger, but he was still in very perilous circumstances. If he moved his right hand from its neck for a moment, the snake, by avoiding suffocation, could easily muster sufficient power to force its head out of his hand: and, if he withdrew his hand from its jaws, he would be fatally in the power of its most dreaded fangs. He retained, therefore, his hold with both his hands. He drew its body between his thighs, in order to aid the compression, and hasten suffocation. Suddenly, the snake, which had remained quiescent for a few moments, brought up its tail, hit him violently on the head, and then darted its body several times very tightly

around his waist. Now was the very acmè of his danger. Thinking, therefore, that he had sufficient power over its body, he withdrew his right hand from its neck, and took (the work of a moment) his large sailor's knife out of his hat. He bent its head on his knee, and, again recommended himself fervently to Heaven, cut its head from its body, throwing the head a great distance. The blood spouted violently in his face; the snake compressed its body still tighter, and Jervas growing black in the face, thought he should be suffocated on the spot, and laid himself down. The snake again rattled its tail, and lashed his feet with it. Gradually, however, he found the animal relax its hold; it soon fell slack around him, and untwisting it, and throwing it from him as far as he was able, he sank down and swooned upon the bank. Some of the natives coming by, and seeing the snake, but not noticing its head was cut off, and Jervas motionless, concluded that he was killed. However, they saw at last the condition of the snake, and that Jervas was recovering a little; they gave him a little rum, unbuttoned his shirt, and by friendly aid in a very short time he recovered, and returned to his vessel, fervently praising the Almighty for his wondrous deliverance.

Terrific Visitation At Sea

Captain Neville Frowde says we reckoned ourselves abreast of the Caribbee Islands and in longitude 54° 0' west of London, when, all of a sudden, about the hour of midnight, it being my watch upon deck, we heard a dismal crack, followed with shower, as it were, of fire, which broke over us, as if the dissolution of the world was coming on; I was struck down, and remained insensible for some time; but when I recovered, found myself, through mercy, unhurt; but three of my watch were killed, and another very much scorched, and those that thus dismally lost their lives, seemed to be reduced to a perfect cinder, and all the buckles, buttons, and every thing else of metal which they had about them were melted. Our main top gallant mast was split to pieces, and our main mast much shattered, our pumps were split, and one of them burst between decks, four of our lower deck planks were torn up, and our main wale burst through about two feet above water, and the ship filled with a sulphurous smoke. The horrid crack which preceded all this, was of no longer duration than whilst a man could count twenty. Such an extraordinary sudden explosion, as it may be called, was hardly ever experienced, and the oldest navigator amongst us, never heard the like in these seas. The captain and my brother officers, were in an instant upon deck, where, the first sight that presented, was me, lying on the quarter deck motionless. At this sight the former broke out in loud lamentations, crying, 'Oh! heavens, he is dead! I have lost my son!' and throwing himself down on me, with his warm pressure restored me to myself, and then his joy was exquisite as his grief had been, at which I testified, a true filial gratitude. We all lamented the unhappy accident, and buried our deceased companions, with decent ceremony, myself being chaplain upon the occasion, and reading the burial service as we committed their bodies to the deep.

Surprising Discovery Of Murder

So many authentic narratives have been given concerning the Welch lights, that none but the sceptical or incredulous can call their existence in question. These are candles or torches, which are sometimes seen over the house of the sick, and are always sure prognostics of death. They have likewise been seen on other extraordinary occasions, as will appear from the following account, the truth of which is known to many in the north of Wales, where this remarkable event came to pass.

A farmer happening to be overtaken by a violent storm of hail and rain, near the hut of a poor labourer, who lived not far from Rhytwin in North Wales, stopped at it, in order to take shelter. The storm continuing, the labourer offered the farmer a bed, which the latter, being very much fatigued, gladly accepted. No sooner was the farmer fast asleep, but the labourer, who conjectured that he must have a considerable sum of money about him, murdered his guest, and taking the money, which amounted to twenty pounds, buried the body on a rising ground behind the hut; and early the next morning went off to Bristol.

The hut was soon after taken by another labourer, who late in the evening after observed a light, which settled constantly on the same spot on the eminence; sometimes there appeared two together, which after blazing a considerable time, suddenly disappeared, and left him filled with terror and consternation. He apprehended that this appearance signified that he was soon to die, and in the anxiety of mind, he imparted what he had seen to three of his acquaintances at Rhytwin, and begged that they would go with him to his hut that evening, that their own eyes might convince them of the truth of what he told them, as they seemed backwards to give credit to an account so extraordinary.

They accordingly went with him to the hut, and after waiting some time, saw, with astonishment, a light settle over the rising ground, and in about ten minutes disappear. They were greatly puzzled to guess at the meaning of this; when at last one of them recollected, that the night before Morgan (that was the name of the murderer) left the country, he happened to pass his hut, and saw a traveller enter. This circumstance made him form a suspicion that a murder had been committed; he therefore advised to dig up the rising ground, at the place over which the light had appeared. This was accordingly done, and the body being quickly found, put murder out of all manner of doubt. Those who had found the body deposed all they knew concerning it before a magistrate at Rhytwin. The coroner sat upon it, and brought in his verdict, 'Wilful Murder.'

As Morgan had been seen at Bristol by some of the inhabitants of Rhytwin, after he left Wales, two constables were dispatched to that city in quest of him. Being taken, he was brought back to Rhytwin, and tried at the ensuing assizes, where there appeared such strong circumstances that he was condemned to die. He however persisted in making the strongest asseverations of his innocence, and kneeling down in open court, prayed to God that his legs might rot off if he was guilty of the murder.

Between the time of his sentence and execution, they in fact rotted off a little below the knees. The hand of God was so visible in this judgement, that the criminal confessed his guilt, and was executed, pursuant to his sentence. This extraordinary event, which happened in the year 1627, may be depended upon as authentic.

The Catacombs Of Kiev

Kiev is a large town, well built, populous, finely situated, and the chief of the district of the same name. We notice that part of Kiev which is more especially indicative of decay, and we therefore quote this account of the catacombs: 'The preparation for descending into this repository of the dead was more solemn than the scene itself; for the monk accompanying us, related such incredible and ridiculous stories of the saints whose relics lay there, that we must have had a more than common share of credulity to have believed them. Every person going down into these vaults purchases a wax taper, and having lighted it, in solemn silence follows the monk, who, as he conducts the visitors through these vaulted sepulchres of the dead, opens the coffin lid, unfolds the shroud, and tells the name of the saint enshrined in that repository: no part of the body is to be seen, of course the flesh is all wasted, and the bones only remain perfect, from having been completely kept from the air; the face and hands are commonly covered with gold or silver tissue, or brocade; a cap is placed on the head, of the same material. Several cells are shewn, where they say monks, in a vow of penance, have had themselves walled up, and only a little window left, at which they received their bread and water, and there remained until their deaths: in one of the cells are twelve masons who built the church, and then entered as monks into the monastery.

'In another place you are shewn the body, or rather the head and shoulders of a man stuck in ground: in a vow of penance he dug a hole, in which he placed himself, standing with his hands by his sides, and then had the hole filled, so that only his head, and a little below the shoulders, could be seen: here he lived, they say, fifteen years, having food and drink brought to him, and a lamp constantly burning by his side: they still allow him a lamp, which burns day and night continually, though he has been dead six or seven hundred years; this, however, they can well afford to do, as he brings a considerable share of the riches of the convent. The cap he wears is supposed to work miracles, and restore the sick; accordingly, hundreds come to visit St. Antonia, and wear his cap, which is frequently the undoubted means of restoring health, though not in the way that enthusiasm and credulity imagine, but by the simple process of being the cause of their taking unusual exercise in the open air, and exercising also a temperance not habitual to them.

I should not omit to mention that St. Antonia is said to sink a little lower in the ground every year, and that the world is to be at an end by the time he entirely disappears. Amongst the wonders which they relate, this can be scarcely be classed as the greatest; and if time in its mighty charges does not annihilate the monastery of Pestcherskey, St. Antonia will probably not disappear, while he continues so instrumental in the well-doing of his brethren.

'Having so particularly mentioned the merits of this saint, let me do justice to the others also, and state, that all have their votaries, and that money lay scattered in every coffin, as if the golden age had returned, and man no longer continued to heap sordid gold, or require its aid to help him to the comforts of life. It is reckoned that from sixty to a hundred thousand pilgrims, from all parts of the Russian empire, visit the monastery at Kiev, in one year: and the revenue the monks derive from the sale of wax candles, is alone sufficient to furnish food for the establishment.'

Giants

Artacaeas, of the family of the Achaemenidae, a person in great favour with Xerxes, was the tallest man of the rest of the Persians; for he lacked but the breath of four fingers of five full cubits by the royal standard, which in our measure must be near seven feet.

Walter Parsons, born in Staffordshire, was first apprentice to a smith, when he grew so tall, that a hole was made for him in the ground, to stand therein up to his knees, so as to make him adequate with his fellow workmen; he afterwards was porter to king James; because gates being generally higher than the rest of the building, it was proper that the porter should be taller than other persons. He was proportionable in all parts, and had strength equal to his height, valour equal to his strength, and good temper equal to his valour; so that he distained to do an injury to any single person; he would take two of the tallest yeomen of the guard in his arms at once, and order them as he pleased. He was seven feet four inches in height.

William Evans was born in Monmouthshire, and may justly be counted the giant of his age; for his stature being full two yards and a half in height, he was porter to king Charles the First, succeeding Walter Parsons in his place, and exceeding him two inches in stature; but he was far beneath him in equal proportion of bone; for he was not only knock-kneed and splay footed, but also halted a little; yet he made a shift to dance in an anti-mask at court, where he drew little Jeffery the king's dwarf out of his pocket, to the no small wonder and laughter of the beholders.

Miracles

A true miracle was performed by Dr Connell, of Bunno, in the county of Cavan, in the year 1777. In the year 1773, about the month of February, a girl of the name of Anne Mulligan, who lived near Roxberry, and who was about fourteen years of age, went over to a neighbour's house on a visit one evening, and returned about ten o'clock at night, having completely lost her speech, and remained in that state till May, 1777, being a space of four years and about a quarter, when her friends brought her to Dr Connell, generally called the 'mad doctor', who, when he had examined the girl and heard the story, brought her into his parlour, and locked the door. Then placing her on a chair on one end of the table, and himself opposite to her at the other, he commenced by distorting his countenance in a shocking manner, so as to strike terror into the girl, and after some time he furiously bounced up, flew to a dagger, which was hanging over the chimney-piece, ran at the girl, swearing he would instantly put her to death, when she dropped on her knees, and exclaimed for God's sake to spare her life, and immediately fainted. On her recovering from the faint, she had completely regained her speech, nor ever after lost it. This can be attested by above twenty persons, and by the tradition of the whole neighbourhood.

Extraordinary Death of M. Foscue, A Miser

Monsieur Foscue, one of the farmers-general of the province of Languedoc, in France, who had amassed considerable wealth in grinding the faces of the poor within his province, by which he rendered himself universally hated, was one day ordered by the government to raise a considerable sum; upon which, as an excuse for not complying with the demand, he pleaded extreme poverty; but, fearing lest some of the inhabitants of Languedoc should give information to the contrary, and his house in consequence be searched, he resolved on hiding his treasure in such a manner as to escape the most strict examination.

He built a kind of cave in his wine cellar, which he made so large and deep, that he used to go down to it with a ladder; at the entrance was a door with a spring lock on it, which on shutting would close itself. Some time after, Monsieur Foscue being missing, diligent search was made after him in every place, and every method which human imagination could suggest was taken for finding him, but all in vain.

In a short time after his death his house was sold, and the purchaser being eager to rebuild it, or make some alterations in it, the workmen discovered a door in the cellar, with a key in the lock, which he ordered to be opened, and on going down they found Monsieur Foscue lying dead on the ground, with a candlestick near him, but no candle in

it, which he had doubtless eaten; and on searching further they found the vast treasure he had amassed. It is supposed, that when Monsieur Foscue went into his cave, the door by some accident shut after him, and being out of the call of any person, he perished for want of food. He had gnawed the flesh off both his arms and shoulders, for subsistence; and the other parts of his body were shrivelled up to that degree, that every bone protruded some distance beyond the covering of the skin.—Thus did this miser die in the midst of his treasure, to the scandal of himself, and the prejudice of the state.

Singular Marriage

Extract from the Parish Register of St Martin, Leicester, February 15, 1576. 'Thomas Tisley and Ursula Russet were married, and because the said Thomas was, and is, naturally deaf and dumb, he could not for his part observe the orders of the form of marriage, after the approbation, had from Thomas, the Bishop of Lincoln, John Chippendale, LL. D and Commissary, and Mr Richard Davis, Mayor of Leicester, and others of his brethren, with the rest of the parish, the said Thomas, for expressing his mind, instead of words, of his own accord used these signs: first, he embraced her with his arms; then he took her by the hand, and put a ring on her finger, and laid his hands upon his heart, then held up his hands to heaven; and to shew his continuance to dwell with her to his life's end, he did it by closing his eyes with his hands, and digging the earth with his feet, and pulling as though he would ring a bell, with other signs approved.'

Combat Between A Bull And A Bear

Raymond says that once, in the Canton of Uri, a bull went in pursuit of a bear, and did not return. After searching for him three successive days, he was found motionless, squeezing against a rock his enemy, who had been long dead, was quite stiff and cold, and almost crushed to pieces by the pressure. Such had been the efforts of the bull, that his feet were deep sunk into the ground.

Remarkable Accident

A singular circumstance took place in the year 1820 at the Comedie Francaise:

Baptiste, who was playing the part of a bailiff, drew from his pocket a paper to represent the warrant by virtue of which he exercised his authority. What was his astonishment on reading the name of one of his female relations, who, through ignorance of a will which had been made in her favour at Dresden, was deprived of a considerable fortune bequeathed to her by her uncle. The paper was a true copy of this will.

Baptiste uttered several exclamations of surprise, accompanied by such comic gesticulations, that the theatre resounded with applause. The audience, however, were far from suspecting the real cause. Baptiste having carefully deposited the paper in his pocket, continued his part, and the next day communicated his discovery to his relation, whose claims were shortly after acknowledged.

This strange adventure is explained as follows: some time before, a party of the performers of the Comedie Francaise proceeded to Dresden, to play in the presence of the sovereigns, who were assembled in that city. Among other scenic accessories, they found it necessary to procure a number of old parchments; and it is probable the document in question remained ever since in the pocket of the dress worn by Baptiste when he made the fortunate discovery.

Terrific Death Of A Painter

Peter Peutemann was a good painter of still-life; but a most memorable circumstance relating to this artist was the incident which occasioned his death. He was employed to paint a picture of an emblematical representation of mortality, expressive of the pleasure of this world, and of the shortness and misery of human life; and that he might imitate some parts of subject with greater accuracy, he painted them in an anatomical room, where several skulls and bones lay scattered in profusion about the floor. Here he prepared to take his designs; and, either from previous fatigue, or the intenseness of his study, he fell asleep. This was on September 18, 1692, when an earthquake, which happened while he was dozing, roused him, and the instant he awoke he perceived the skulls rolling about the room, and the skeletons in motion! Being totally ignorant of the cause, he was struck with such horror, that he immediately threw himself down stairs in the wildest desperation. His friends took all possible pains to efface the dreadful impression from his mind, explaining the true cause of the agitation of the skeletons; nevertheless, his spirits received so violent a shock, that he never recovered his health, but expired soon after, aged forty-two.

A Narrow Escape

The hero of this history, was a native of Rimini, a city in the papal territory, and a very accomplished gentleman, his name was Signior Pandolfo. He had served some years in the French king's armies, and with reputation. He had retired some time afterwards, resolving to pass the reminder of his years in his native soil. He was then about thirty-six, and as active and sprightly as when he was a lad. It so happened that his house joined to that of an old gentleman who had married a young wife, the daughter of a man of great quality, tough but of mean fortune.

Signior Pandolfo had not long been at home when this lady cast her eyes upon him. She was a woman addicted to pleasure, and without any regard for the laws of honour or religion. She made therefore no manner of scruple of acquainting Signior Pandolfo with her kindness for him; and he, much too fine a gentleman to feel any restraint from conscience, contrived a method for their better acquaintance, by breaking a passage into her maid's chamber, whence he was easily conducted to her's.

But to prevent all possibility of surprise, the lady caused several holes to be bored in a very large chest, where she kept her choicest clothes and her jewels which was all the fortune she brought her husband, that upon any emergency Pandolfo might be locked up therein, and yet not suffer for want of air.

Things went on this course for about two years, when the lady fell dangerously ill. Finding her end approach, she would needs take leave of Pandolfo; but in the midst of this interview, hearing her husband coming, he was forced to betake himself to this chest, in which he had not lain long before he heard the lady address herself in these words. 'My tenderly loving and much-beloved lord, I find life retiring; gratify me in one request dying, to whom living you denied nothing.' 'Speak,' said the good old man, 'and be assured, that whatever you ask shall be granted.' 'Let then,' said she, 'that chest be set upon my coffin without any body being suffered to look on it.' 'It shall be so,' replied the husband. Presently some of her relations came to visit her, and in a couple of hours she expired.

As her distemper was a kind of malignant fever, it was resolved to bury her about midnight of the next day, which was accordingly done, and the chest unopened, placed upon her coffin in the vault where she was intended. Before her amour with Signior Pandolfo, she had shewn some marks of favour to her husband's page, who had thereby an opportunity of seeing the jewels that were in her chest. This man conceiving that such things were of little use to the dead, went to the sexton, and having promised him and his son a share in the booty, prevailed on them to take a share in the enterprise of searching the chest.

Signior Pandolfo, in the meantime, gave himself up for dead, and besought the Almighty to pardon him in his manifold sins, and to suffer them to be expiated in the cruel punishment. Such were his meditations when he heard the door of the vault open, and soon after found them tampering about the lock of the chest. Conceiving thereupon a sudden hope of deliverance, he pushed back the spring of the lock, and throwing up the lid of the chest, started up all at once.

The thieves, supposing it was the devil come to punish them for their sacrilegious attempt, fled without looking behind them. Pandolfo having put as many of the jewels as he thought fit into his pockets, went and hid himself in a private part of the church till morning, and then retired to his own house secretly. His son, for he afterwards married, being a priest in the fortieth year of his age, retired to Geneva, where he became a Protestant, married a young woman, and left a numerous family.

Wonderful Providence

The following singular account is related by Thuanus in his History of the civil wars of France. When the Catholics besieged Rouen, in the year 1562 (a period of time rendered remarkable on account of the civil wars which originated from religious disputes), Francis Civile, a gentleman of the Calvinist party, received a wound, which made him fall senseless from the ramparts of the town. Some soldiers, who believed him dead, stripped and buried him with the negligence usual on such occasions. An affectionate servant whom he had retained in his service, desirous of giving his master a more honourable burial, went with a design to find his remains. His search being fruitless among so many dead bodies, he covered them again with earth, but so that the hand of one of them remained uncovered. As he was retiring, he happened to look behind him, and perceived the hand, and fearing that the object might incite dogs to unearth the body to devour it, he returned in order to cover it, when the light of the moon just emerging from a cloud discovered to him a diamond ring on the finger, which he knew to be Civile's. Without delay he took up his master, who had just breath in him, and carried him to the hospital of the wounded; but the surgeons being fatigued with labour, and considering him on the point of death, took no trouble with his wounds. The servant found himself obliged to take him to his own house, where he laid for four days without any help. At the end of that time two physicians visited him, and by their care and attention he was placed in a fair way of recovery. The town having been taken by assault, the conquerors had the barbarity to throw him out of the window. He fortunately fell on a heap of dung, where, abandoned by every one, he lay three days in the most miserable condition. Du Croiset, his relation, had him carried off in the middle of the night, and sent to a house in the country, where his wounds were dressed, and he completely recovered. Civile lived forty years after this event in perfect health.

That particular Providence which had saved this man from so many perils had also presided over his birth. His mother dying with child in the absence of his father, had been buried without any one thinking of extracting the infant by the Caesarian operation. The day after she was interred, the husband arrived, and learned with the greatest surprise and sorrow, the death of his wife, and the little attention that had been paid to the fruit of her womb. He had her immediately dug up, opened, and extracted Civile still living!

Courageous Indifference

At the battle of Fontenoy, an officer of the name of Honeywood was endeavouring to cleave down a French soldier, but his hanger sticking in his shoulder, the fellow gained strength enough to run him through the side with his bayonet, while another struck him on the head and face with a sabre, so that he immediately fell. Next day Lord Robert Manner, looking at the wagons that were carrying off the wounded, beheld Honeydew on one of them, with half a dozen soldiers lying on the top of them – 'Poor fellow!' said his lordship, 'thou art now done for, sure enough!' But what was his surprise when, on arriving at Hannau, he received a message with 'Mr Honeywood's compliments,' desiring him to go and see his wounds dressed. He went directly – 'And now Bob,' said the gallant creature, 'look sharp, and thou shalt see my brains, and Middleton, the surgeon here, shall testify that I have some.'

A Dream Fatally Fulfilled

A man dreaming that he was torn in pieces by a lion, and looking upon it as a chimera resulting from the confused and disturbed actions of mind and body in a dream when fancy predominates over reason, slighted it; and the next day seeing the figure of a lion cut in stone, supported by pillars, he told those who were walking with him what he had dreamed, and merrily thrust his hand into the lion's jaw, saying, 'Now bite me if thou canst!' He had no sooner spoken the words but a scorpion, which had taken up its lodging in the lion's mouth, stung him in the hand; which poisonous wound resisting all applications proved his death.

God's Vengeance On Forestallers Of Corn

In the year 1434, says Matthew Paris, was a great dearth and scarcity of corn throughout the whole kingdom, but more especially in the northern parts of it. For three years after a great mortality raged: multitudes died of pestilence as well as of famine; the great men at that time taking no care to relieve them. Archbishop Walter Grey had then in granaries and elsewhere a stock of corn, which if delivered out, would have supplied the country for five years. But whether they did not offer him price enough, or for some other reasons, he would not part with a grain of it. At length being told that the corn stacks and other ricks would suffer for want of thrashing, being apt to be consumed by mice and other vermin, he ordered that it should be delivered to the husbandmen who dwelt upon his manors, upon condition they should pay him as much new corn for it after harvest.

Accordingly some of his officers went to Ripon, where his largest stores were deposited, and coming to a great stack to take it down, they saw the heads of many snakes, adders, toads, and other venomous creatures peeping out at the end of the sheaves. This being told to the archbishop, he sent his steward and others of good credit to enquire into the truth of it, who finding it true, would nevertheless force some of the countrymen to mount to the top with ladders, and throw down some of the sheaves. They had no sooner ascended, but a thick black smoke seemed to arise from the midst of the corn, which made such an intolerable stench, that it soon obliged the husbandmen to come down again, declaring they never smelt any thing like it before.

As they descended, they heard a voice say, 'Let the corn alone, for the archbishop and all that belongs to him is the devil's due.'

In short, they were obliged to build a wall about the stack, and set it on fire, lest such a number of venomous creatures should get out and infest the whole country.

Extraordinary Experiment

About 1776, there appeared an account from Port St Louis, in Brittany, in France, of a galley-slave who had been condemned to death for murder, but who was promised life and liberty, and a considerable reward, upon condition of suffering himself to be dressed in a certain apparatus, and pushed off the top of building seventy feet high, for the purpose of ascertaining the power of air in supporting a superincumbent weight.

A further experiment, with some improvements, was made in the presence of many persons of distinction. A gentleman who is extremely curious in every branch of mechanics and natural philosophy, having written to a friend to Nantes, relative to the affair, received the following account: 'The slave in question, whose name was Dominic Dufour, aged about twenty-four years, on the morning of the 29th of September, ascended to the leads of the Arsenal, one hundred and forty-five feet, from the terrace of the Esplanade, dressed in a suit of feathered tissue, accompanied by the Duke D'Aiguilon, Governor of Brittany, the Abbé de Henry, and the King's Professor of Mathematics in the Academy of Rennes. A strong cephalic cordial being given him, he was pushed very gently off the parapet of the building, in sight of more than ten thousand spectators; and after fluttering a little in a brisk wind, began to descend, in a steady uniform manner, at a distance of about ten feet from the wall of the tower, amidst the acclamations of the people, whose joy for his success would have been immoderate, if not checked by some anxiety for the event; which soon relived them, for the successful convict alighted upon his feet in perfect safety, being exactly two minutes and thirteen seconds in his descent. He was immediately let blood, and conducted through the principal streets, with drums and trumpets, to the Town Hall, where the magistrates gave a splendid entertainment to many nobility and others, who came from all parts of the country to behold the extraordinary sight. A handsome collection was made by the company, and the prisoner relieved, with a certificate of his performance, to entitle him to the king's bounty and most gracious pardon, with which he set off the next day to Paris. M. Defontagne, who is the author of this invention, has applied for an exclusive patent for his natural life, as such an apparatus may be of invaluable consequence in cases of sudden accident, particularly fire, for which purpose it was chiefly intended.'

Ferocity Of Wolves In India

When a wolf enters a camp or village, he proceeds with the utmost silence and circumspection. His favourite object is a child at the breast; which, when opportunity serves, he seizes by the throat, thereby not only preventing it from giving an alarm by its cries, but taking a hold which enables him to bear away his prize without impeding its progress. He will thus carry it through the crowds who, at the first notice, rush from all quarters to intercept him in his flight. Often when closely pursued, especially if hit by a stick or stone, he will drop the child; but if not taken away immediately, the ferocious brute will sometimes make a turn on the spot, and snap it up again. Few children survive the bite; and many grown persons carry the marks of wolves' teeth.

Troops in general move with a host of camp-followers; many of them having families. Numbers of young children, especially such as, being at the breast, cannot be sent by water necessarily accompany. In many parts of the country, especially in the dominions of the Nabob Vizier of Oude, all are kept in a continual state of alarm. When a wolf is seen by the sentries, who dare not fire among such crowds, a general shout and pursuit immediately takes place. Yet it often happens that three or four young children are carried off, or at least seized and dropped, in the course of a night. Many are taken from the arms of their mothers, though covered with quilts, and surrounded perhaps by a dozen persons, who take every possible precaution, except that of watching, for the preservation of the infants.

The wolf proceeds in so subtle a manner, that often a child is taken from its mother's breast, and not missed until the beating of the drums may rouse the whole camp for the purpose of marching, when the parent first becomes acquainted with her loss. The melancholy effect produced by the cries of mothers whose children have been purloined, and to whom no kind of aid can avail, nor consolation be administered, surpasses imagination. They continue to distress the feeling of all during the whole night, and occasion reflections that debar the mind endued with sensibility from enjoying a moment's repose.

Two wolves succeeded in getting into the area of a bungalow occupied by Lieutenant Colonel Powel, then post-master at Cawnpore, where they found a lad of about thirteen years of age, a relation of the family, asleep. They soon killed him with their usual manner of seizing the throat, after which they dragged him carefully to the foot of the wall. The falling of a tile from the coping created an alarm, when the wolves were discovered, one standing on his hind legs the fore feet resting against the wall, and holding up the lad by the throat; the other wolf on the wall, leaning down as much as he could in the endeavour to obtain a hold so as to drag him over. Human ingenuity could scarcely have devised better means from accomplishing such a purpose. It is to be observed that in every respect but the seizure of the throat there was no

mark or bite about the unfortunate youth. The wolves, no doubt, expected to succeed in getting him over the wall, when they would have begun that ceremony, which they feared might have been too eagerly performed, within the premises, and baulked them of their meal.

During the time above noticed, the wolves had become extremely bold. Till then they had rarely been known to attack adult persons. Finding so many to become an easy prey, they either lost the power of discrimination, or from that audacity so often attendant upon success, so little attended to the age, sex, or station of such persons as fell in their way, that numbers of the stoutest men in our camps were attacked, and many of them killed sometimes by a single wolf; though they were generally observed to be two or three in company. An European sentry was taken from his post; and a sepoy who was sent as guard to some people employed to cut grass for thatches from Jooey plain, was attacked at mid-day by several wolves. He destroyed five with his arms, and probably would have got rid of some others that remained, had not one of them, going round to his back, sprung upon his neck, and brought him to the ground, when the poor fellow was soon torn to pieces.

The Water Drinkers

The following astonishing instances of extreme thirst are extracted from the 'Morning Chronicle' of July, 1814.

Catherine Beausergent has been distinguished from her most tender age, by a thirst, which nothing could quench. In her infancy, she drank two pailsfull of water every day. When her parents endeavoured to prevent her drinking water so abundantly, she procured it clandestinely; in summer, from the river, and from the houses of neighbours, even in the streets; and in winter, from pieces of ice, or from snow, which she melted privately, night and day. The harsh manner in which her family treated her on account of this propensity, induced her at length, to quit her paternal mansion. She went to Paris, and entered into the service of some friends more indulgent than her parents, and who left her at liberty to drink as much water as she chose. Her conduct in this service was irreproachable. At twenty-two years of age, she was married to a man named Ferry, a cordwainer, from whom she concealed her ardent thirst, though fear that he would not espouse her. She had nine children in 1789. During the months she was in the family way, her thirst increased: she refused constantly to quench it with any other drink than fresh water, of which she drank three or four pints at one time. In the winter of 1788, being then near her time of delivery, she drank nearly two pailsfull of water in twenty-four hours; water at that time cost six sous per pail. Her husband went for snow and ice, and thawed it. Extraordinarily, she could never drink a glass of wine without pain and shivering.

The Journal Etranger, 1753, mentions a young woman, aged twenty years, felt for fourteen years a great desire for thirst. She drank usually in twenty-four hours, eighteen to twenty pints of water; from six to twenty years, she had drunk 95,000 pints of water.

Extraordinary Female Duel

The duke of Richelieu was the cause of an unprecedented duel between two females, Madame de Polignac and Madame de Nesle, who disputed the possession of him. The duke had repeatedly refused to see the former, but this was of no avail. Madame de Polignac still loved her inconstant gallant with as much ardour as ever, and was therefore jealous of all the ladies that had succeeded her, not singly, but in troops. Tortured by jealousy, she one day met Madame de Nesle, and challenged her to fight with pistols in the Bois de Boulonge. Madame de Nesle eagerly accepted the challenge, being animated by the same spirit as her fair antagonist, and hoping either to kill her antagonist, and thus remain in undisturbed possession of her lover, or to evince the strength of her attachment, and the ardour of her passion, by an honourable death. The ladies met, and fired at each other. Madame de Nesle fell, and her fair bosom was covered with blood. 'Come on,' exclaimed her antagonist, 'I will teach you the consequences of robbing a woman like me of her lover; if I had the perfidious creature in my power I would tear out her heart as I have blown out her brains.'

A young man, who had heard these cruel words, begged her to moderate herself, and not exult over her unfortunate opponent, whose courage, at least, could not but command her respect. 'Silence, young coxcomb,' cried Madame de Polignac, 'it does not become you to give me instruction.'

Madame de Nesle had not been wounded in the breast, as had at first been feared, but very slightly in the shoulder. On coming to herself, some person asked her if the lover, for whose sake she had fought, was worth her exposing herself to such risk for him? 'Oh yes,' replied she, 'he deserves much better blood than what circulates in my veins to be shed for him. He is the most amiable man of the whole court; all the ladies lay snares for him; but I hope, after this proof of love which I have given, to obtain the exclusive possession of his heart. I am under too great obligations to you,' continued she, 'to conceal his name – it is the duke de Richelieu; yes, the duke de Richelieu, the first-born of the God of War and the Goddess of Love.'

An Archer's Revenge

Philip, king of Macedon, lost one of his eyes by a very singular accident. Besieging the small city of Methone, a man named Aster, of Amphipolis, offered his services to Philip, telling him he was so excellent a marksman, that he could bring down birds in their most rapid flight. The monarch made this answer, 'Well, then, I will take you into my service when I make war upon starlings.' This reply stung the archer to the quick, and here it was fully proved, that a repartee may be of fatal consequences to him who makes it. Aster, having thrown himself into the city, let fly an arrow, on which was written, 'To Philip's right eye.' This carried a most cruel proof that he was a good marksman, for he actually hit him in the right eye. Philip, however, sent him back the arrow, with this inscription; 'If Philip takes Methone, he will hang up Aster;' and accordingly, having taken it, he was as good as his word.

Singular Phenomenon

There have been, at different periods of time, very remarkable instances of the convulsions of nature, but there are few recorded equal to the following.

In the month of April, 1793, the waters of the River de la Plata were forced, by a most violent current of wind, to the distance of ten leagues, so that the bed of the river was left quite dry. A number of ships, which had been sunk in the river for upwards of thirty years, were uncovered, and amongst others, an English vessel, which was cast away in the year 1762. Several persons repaired to the bed of the river, on which they could walk almost without wetting their feet, and returned laden with silver and other riches, which had long been buried under water. This phenomenon, which may be long ranked among the grand revolutions of nature, continued three days, at the end of which the wind ceased, and the water returned with great violence to its natural bed.

Youthful Heroism

In the engagement of Ushant, on the memorable fatal July 27th, 1779, a boy in the Formidable had his arm shot away, and of course he was taken to the cock-pit. There he got himself dressed; but finding his heart glow with British courage, he stole up to the very same gun where he had received the accident. Sir Hugh Palliser, perceiving him, called out and asked why he did not remain below. The boy replied, 'D——n my eyes she an't struck yet, and I'll not quit my post while I can.' At that moment a ball struck him in the belly, and tore him in the most shocking manner. He was then carried down, and contrary to the opinion of the surgeon, and all who saw his situation, he recovered. Sir Hugh, when the fleet returned, made the young hero a present of ten guineas, and telling the story to Lord Sandwich, his lordship settled on him an annuity of twenty pounds per annum, and he afterward resided in his native place, Shoreditch. What is very remarkable, he, a short time after, presented a petition to the Admiralty, praying to be rated on board the Grand Fleet, alledging that though he wanted an arm and part of his belly, he was ten times better, and would be of more use on board, than any fresh water sailor that their lordships might employ.

Family Escape

In September, 1789, a little boy, about five years old, the son of a man named Freemantle, in St Thomas's Church-yard, Salisbury, being at play by the dam of the two mills, fell into the water; his sister, a child nine years of age, instantly plunged in to his assistance. They both sunk, and in sight of their mother! The poor woman, distracted with horror at the prospect of the instant death of the children, braved the flood to save them; she rose with one under each arm, and by her cries happily alarmed her husband, who instantly swam to her assistance, and brought them all three safe ashore.

Fatal Conceit

Marcus Donatus, in his Hist. Med. Rar. records the case of a person of the name of Vincentinus, who believed that he was of such enormous size, that he could not go through the door of his apartment. His physician gave orders that he should be forcibly led through it; which was done accordingly, but not without fatal effect, for Vincentinus cried out, as he was forced along, that the flesh was torn from his bones, and that his limbs were broken off; of which terrible impression he died a few days after, accusing those who conducted him of being his murderers.

The Rightful Heir Restored

A jeweller who carried on an extensive trade, and supplied the deficiencies of one country by the superfluities of another, leaving his home with a valuable assortment of diamonds, for a distant region, took with him his son, and a young slave, whom he had purchased in his infancy, and brought up more like an adopted child, than a servant. They performed their intended journey, and the merchant disposed of his commodities with great advantage; but while preparing to return, he was seized by a pestilential distemper, and died suddenly in the metropolis of a foreign country.

This accident inspired the slave with a wish to possess his master's treasures, and relying on the total ignorance of strangers, and the kindness every where shewn him by the jeweller, he declared himself the son of the deceased, and took charge of his property. The true heir of course denied his pretensions, and solemnly declared himself to be the only son of the defunct, who had long before purchased his opponent as a slave. This contest produced various opinions. It happened that the slave was a young man of comely person, and of polished manners; while the jeweller's son was ill-favoured by nature, and still more injured in his education, by the indulgence of his parents. This superiority operated in the minds of many to support the claims of the former; but since no certain evidence could be produced on either side, it became necessary to refer the dispute to a court of law. There, however, from a total want of proofs, nothing could be done.

The magistrate declared his inability to decide on unsupported assertions, in which each party was equally positive. This caused a report of the case to be made to the prince, who having heard the particulars, was also confounded, and at a loss how to decide the question.

At length, a happy thought occurred to the chief of judges, and he engaged to ascertain the real heir. The two claimants being summoned before him, he ordered them to stand behind a curtain prepared for the occasion, and to project their heads through two openings, when, after hearing their several arguments, he would cut off the head of him who should prove to be the slave. This they readily assented to; the one from a reliance on his honesty, the other from a confidence of the impossibility of detection. Accordingly, each taking his place as ordered, thrust his head through a hole in the curtain. An officer stood in front with a drawn sword in his hand, and the Judge proceeded to the examination. After a short debate, the Judge cried out, 'Enough, enough, strike off the villain's head!' and the officer, who watched the moment, leaped toward the two youths; the impostor, startled at the brandished weapon, hastily drew back his head, while the jeweller's son, animated by conscious security, stood unmoved. The Judge immediately decided for the latter, and ordered the slave to be taken into custody, to receive the punishment due to his diabolical ingratitude.

Ingenious Device

The French police being unable to discover any traces of the perpetrator of a very extraordinary robbery at Lyons, in the year 1780, resorted to the expedient of sending an officer to the Bicetre, disguised as a prisoner. He acted his part extremely well, and interested his audience highly by his account of the exploit. In this assembly of connoisseurs in guilt, one of them exclaimed, 'It is only Philip who could execute such a stroke.' This led to the discovery, that Philip was in fact the leader of the gang.

Singular Recovery From Apparent Death

A very singular adventure happened to David Beek, the painter, as he travelled through Germany. He was suddenly and violently taken ill at an inn where he lodged, and was laid out as a corpse, seeming to all appearance quite dead. His valets expressed the strongest marks of grief at the loss of their master: and while they sat at the side of his bed, they drank very freely by way of consolation. At last one of them, who grew much intoxicated, said to his companions – 'Our master was fond of his glass while he was alive, and out of gratitude, let us give him a glass now he is dead.' At the rest of the servants assented to his proposal, he raised up the head of his master, and endeavoured to pour some of the liquor into his mouth. By the fragrance of the wine, or probably by a small quantity that imperceptibly got down his throat, Beek opened his eyes; and the servant being excessively drunk, and forgetting that his master was considered as dead, compelled him to swallow what wine remained in the glass. The painter gradually revived, and by proper management and care recovered perfectly, and escaped an interment.

Furious Combat With Bears

The following interesting narrative is extracted from Captains Lewis and Clarke's 'Travels to the source of the

Missouri River, and across the American Continent to the Pacific Ocean, performed by order of the government of the United States, in the years 1804, 1805, 1806.'

'About five in the afternoon one of our men who had been afflicted with biles, and was suffered to walk on shore, came running to the boats with loud cries and every symptom of terror and distress: for some time after we had taken him on board, he was so out of breath as to be unable to describe the cause of his anxiety, but at length told us, that about a mile and a half below he had shot a brown bear, which immediately turned, and was in close pursuit of him; but the bear, being badly wounded, could not overtake him. Captain Lewis, with seven men, immediately went in close pursuit of him, and having found his track, followed him by the blood for about a mile, and finding him concealed in some thick brushwood, shot him with two balls through the skull. Though somewhat smaller than one killed a few days before, he was a monstrous animal and a most terrible enemy; our man had shot him through the centre of the lungs, yet he had pursued him furiously for half a mile then returned more than twice that distance, and with his talons prepared himself a bed in the earth, five feet long and two feet deep, and was perfectly alive when they found him, which was at least two hours after he received the wound. The wonderful power of life which these animals possess renders them dreadful; their very track in the mud or sand, which we found eleven inches long and seven inches and a quarter wide, exclusive of talons, is alarming; and we had rather encounter two Indians than meet one brown bear. There is no chance of killing them by a single shot, unless the ball go through the brains, and this is very difficult on account of two large muscles which cover the side of the forehead, and the sharp projection of the centre of the frontal bone, which is also thick.

Towards evening the men in the hindmost canoes discovered a brown bear lying in the open grounds about three hundred paces from the river. Six of them, all good hunters, immediately went to attack him; and concealing themselves by a small eminence, came unperceived within forty paces of him; four of the hunters now fired, and each lodged a ball in his body, two of them directly through the lungs. The furious animal sprang up, and ran furiously upon them; as he came near, the two hunters who had reserved their fire, gave him two wounds, one of which, breaking his shoulder, retarded his motion for a moment; but before they could reload he was so near them they were obliged to run to the river, and before they reached it he had almost overtaken them: two jumped into the canoe; the other four separated, and concealed themselves in the willows, fired as fast as each could reload; they struck him several times, but instead of weakening the monster, each shot seemed only to direct him towards the hunter, till at last he pursued two of them so closely, that they threw aside their guns and pouches, and jumped down a perpendicular bank of twenty feet into the river; the bear sprang after them, and was within a few feet of the hindmost, when one of the hunters on shore shot him through the head, and finally killed him.'

Terrific Gallantry

After the death of Montezuma, the Mexicans took possession of a high tower in the great temple, which overlooks the Spanish quarters, and placing there a garrison of their principal warriors, not a Spaniard could stir without being exposed to their missile weapons. From this post it was necessary to dislodge them at any risk. Juan de Escobar thrice made the attempt, but was repulsed. Ferdinando Cortes, sensible that not only the reputation, but the safety of his army depended on the success of this assault, ordered a buckler to

be tied to his arm, and rushed with his drawn sword into the thickest of the combatants. Encouraged by the presence of their general, the Spaniards returned to the charge with such vigour, that they gradually forced their way up the steps, and drove the Mexicans to the platform at the top of the tower. There a dreadful carnage began; when two young Mexicans, observing Cortes as he animated his soldiers by his voice and example, resolved to sacrifice their own lives, in order to cut off the author of all the calamities which desolated their country. They approached him in a suppliant posture, as if they had intended to lay down their arms, and seizing him in a moment, hurried him towards the walls, over which they threw themselves headlong, in hopes of dragging him along to be dashed to pieces by the same fall. But Cortes, by his strength and gallantry, broke loose from their grasp; and the gallant youths perished in the generous, though unsuccessful attempt to save their country.

Spontaneous Combustion Of The Human Body

The Countess Cornelia Bandi, of the town of Cesena, aged sixty-two, enjoyed a good state of health. One evening, having experienced a sort of drowsiness, she retired to bed, and her maid remained with her till she fell asleep. Next morning when the girl entered the room to awaken her, she found nothing but the remains of her mistress in a most horrid condition. At a distance of about four feet from the bed was a heap of ashes, in which could be distinguished the legs and the arms untouched. Between the legs lay the head, the brains of which, together with half the posterior part of the cranium, and the whole chin had been consumed; three fingers were found in the state of a coal; the rest of the body was consumed to ashes, and contained no oil; the tallow of two candles were melted on a table, but the wicks still remained, and the feet of the candlesticks were covered with a certain moisture. The bed was not damaged, the bed-clothes and coverlid were raised and thrown on one side, as is the case when a person gets up. The furniture and the tapestry were covered with a moist kind of soot of the colour of ashes, which had penetrated into the drawers, and dirtied the linen. This soot having been conveyed to a neighbouring kitchen, adhered to the walls and utensils. A piece of bread in the cupboard was covered with it, and no dog would touch it. The infectious odour had been communicated to other apartments. The Annual Register states, that the Countess Cesena was accustomed to bathe all her body in camphorated spirit of wine.– This surprising fact was confirmed to the Royal Society of London, by Paul Rolli.

An instance of this kind is preserved in the same work, in a letter of Mr Wilmer, Surgeon,–'Mary Clues, aged fifty years, was much addicted to intoxication. Her propensity to this vice had increased after the death of her husband, which happened a year and a half before; for about a year a day scarcely passed in the course of which she did not drink half a pint of rum or anniseed water. Her health gradually declined, and about the beginning of February she was attacked by jaundice, and confined to her bed. Though she was incapable of much action, and not in a condition to work, she still continued her old habit of drinking and smoking a pipe of tobacco. The bed in which she lay stood parallel to the chimney of the apartment, the distance for it being about three feet. On Saturday morning she fell on the floor, and her extreme weakness preventing her from getting up, she remained in this state till some one entered and put her to bed. The following night she wished to be left alone; a woman quitted her at half-past eleven, and according to custom shut the door and locked it. She had put two large pieces of coal, and placed a light in a candlestick on a chair at the foot of the bed. At half-past five in the morning, a smoke was seen issuing from the windows, and the door being speedily broken open, some flames which were in the room were soon extinguished. Between the bed and the chimney were found the remains of the unfortunate Clues; one leg and a thigh were still entire, but there remained nothing of the skin, the muscles, and the viscera. The bones of the cranium, the breast, the spine, and other extremities were entirely calcined, and covered with a whitish efflorescence. The people were much surprised to find that the furniture had sustained so little injury. The side of the bed which was next to the chimney had suffered most; the wood of it was slightly burnt, but the feather-bed, the clothes and covering were safe. I entered the apartment about two hours after it had been opened, and observed that the wall and every thing in it were blackened, and that it was filled by a very disagreeable vapour; but that nothing except the body exhibited any strong traces of fire.'

This instance has a great similarity to that related by Vicq d'Axyr in the Encyclopedic Methodique, under the head Pathologic Anatomy of Man. A woman, fifty years old, who indulged to excess in spirituous liquors, and got drunk every day before she went to bed, was found entirely burnt and reduced to ashes. Some of the osseous were only left, but the furniture of the apartment had suffered very little damage. Vicq d'Axyr instead of disbelieving this phenomenon, adds, that there have been many other instances of the like kind.

A woman at Paris, who had been accustomed for three years, to drink spirits of wine to such a degree that she used no other liquor, was found one day entirely reduced to ashes, except the skull and the extremities of the fingers.

The transactions of the Royal Society of London present also an instance of human combustion no less extraordinary. It was mentioned at the time it happened in all the journals; it was then attested by a great number of eye-witnesses, and became the subject of many learned discussions. Three accounts of this event, by different authors, all nearly coincide.—'Grace Pitt, the wife of a fishmonger of the parish of St Clement, Ipswich, aged about sixty, had contracted a habit, which she continued for several years, of coming down every night from her bed-room, half dressed to smoke a pipe. On the night of the ninth of April, 1744, she got up from her bed as usual; her daughter, who slept with her, did not perceive that she was absent till the next morning when she awoke, soon after this she put on her clothes, and going down into the kitchen, found her mother stretched out on the right side, with her head near the grate; the body extended on the hearth, with the legs on the floor, which was of deal, having the appearance of a log of wood, consumed by a fire without flame. On beholding this spectacle, the girl ran in great haste and poured over her mother's body some water contained in two large vessels, in order to extinguish the fire; while the fetid odour and smoke which exhaled from the body, almost suffocated some of the neighbours who had hastened to the girl's assistance. The trunk was in some places incinerated, and resembled a heap of coals covered with white ashes. The head, the arms, the legs, and the thighs had participated in the burning. This woman, it is said, had drunk a large quantity of spirituous liquors in consequence of being overjoyed to hear that one of her daughters had returned from Gibraltar. There was no fire in the grate, and the candle had entirely burnt out in the socket of the candlestick, which was close to her. Besides, there was found near the consumed body, the clothes of a child, and a paper screen, which had sustained no injury by the fire. The dress of the woman consisted of a cotton gown.'

Le Cat, in his memoirs, relates another instance: 'M. Boinneau, rector of Plerquer, near Dol,' says he, 'wrote to me the following letter, dated February 22nd, 1749:– Allow me to communicate a fact which took place here about a fortnight ago. Mad. De Boiseon, eighty years of age, exceedingly meagre, who had drunk nothing but spirits for several years, was sitting in her elbow chair before the fire, while her waiting-maid went out of the room a few minutes. On her return, seeing her mistress on fire, she immediately gave an alarm; and some people having come to her assistance, one of them endeavoured to extinguish the flames with his hands, but they adhered to it as if they had been dipped in brandy or oil on fire. Water was brought, and thrown on the lady in abundance; yet the fire appeared more violent, and was not extinguished till the whole flesh had been consumed. Her skeleton, exceedingly black, remained entire in the chair, which was only a little scorched; one leg only, and two hands detached themselves from the rest of the bones. It is not known whether her clothes caught fire by approaching the grate. The lady was in the same place in which she sat every day; there was no extraordinary fire, and she had not fallen. What makes me suppose that the use of spirits might have produced this effect, is, that I have been assured that at the gate of Dinan, an accident of the like kind happened to another woman under similar circumstances.

The following instance, recorded in the Journal de Medicine (vol. lix. P.140.) took place at Caen, and is thus related by Merille, a surgeon of that city. 'Being requested on the third of June, 1782, by the king's officers, to draw up a report of the state in which I found Mademoiselle Thuars, who was said to have been burnt, I made the following observations:— The body lay with the crown of the head resting against one of the end irons, at a distance of eighteen inches from the fire, the remainder of the body was placed obliquely before the chimney, the whole being nothing but a mass of ashes. Even the most solid bones had lost their form and consistence; none of them could be distinguished, except the coronal, the two parietal bones, the two lumber vertebrae, a portion of the tibia, and a part of the omoplate; and even these were so calcined, that they became dust by the least pressure. The right foot was found entire, but scorched at the upper junction; the left was more burnt. The day was cold, and there was nothing in the grate but two or three bits of wood about an inch in diameter, burnt in the middle. None of the furniture in the apartment was damaged. The chair on which Mademoiselle Thuars had been sitting was found at a distance of a foot from her, and absolutely untouched. I must here observe, that the lady was exceedingly corpulent: that she was sixty years of age, and much addicted to spirituous liquors; that on the day of her death she had drunk three bottles of wine and a bottle of brandy; and that the consumption of the body had taken place in less than seven hours, though, according to appearance, nothing around the body was burnt but the clothes.'

Fatal Effects Of Poison

A farmer in Pennsylvania went to mowing, in his boots; a caution used to prevent being stung. Inadvertently he trod on a snake, which immediately flew at his legs; and as it drew back, in order to renew its blow, one of his men cut it to pieces with his scythes. They prosecuted their work, and returned home. At night the farmer pulled off his boots, and went to bed; and was soon attacked with a strange sickness at his stomach. He swelled, and before a physician could be sent for, he died. The sudden death of the man did not cause much inquiry. The neighbourhood wondered, as is usual in such cases, and without further examination the corpse was buried.

A few days after the son put on his father's boots, and went to the meadows; at night he pulled them off, went to bed, and was attacked with the same symptoms in about the same time, and died in the morning. A little before he died the doctor came, but was not able to assign the cause of so singular a disorder. However, rather than appear wholly at a loss before the country people, he pronounced both father and son been bewitched.

Some weeks after the widow sold all the moveables for the benefit of the younger children; and the farm was leased. One of the neighbours, who bought the boots, presently put them on, and was attacked in the very same manner as the other two had been. But this man's wife, being alarmed at what had happened in the former family, dispatched one of the servants for an eminent physician, who fortunately, having heard of the dreadful affair, guessed the cause, applied oil. &c. and recovered the man. The boots, which had been so fatal, were then carefully examined; and found that the two fangs of the snake had been left in the leather, after being wrenched out of their sockets by the strength with which the snake had drawn backs its head. The bladders, which contained the poison, and several of the small nerves, were still fresh, and adhered to the boot. The unfortunate father and son had been poisoned by pulling off the boots, by which action they imperceptibly scratched their legs with the point of the fangs, through the hollow of which some of the poison had been conveyed.

Singular Galvanic Experiments

The term Galvanism is derived from Galvani, a professor of anatomy at Bologna, who, not many years since, discovered a certain influence, or species of electricity, by which animal bodies were strangely affected, by application of metallic substances to particular parts of the nervous system.

Among the numerous experiments which have lately been made, very few have been more singular than those which were produced by Dr Ure, in Glasgow, on the body of a man named Clydesdale, who had been executed for murder. These effects were produced by a Voltaic battery of 270 pair of four-inch plates, of which the results were terrible. In the first experiment, on moving the rod from the thigh to the heel, the leg was thrown forward with such violence, as nearly to overturn one of the assistants. In the second experiment, the rod was applied to the phrenic nerve in the neck, when laborious breathing commenced; the chest heaved and fell; the belly was protruded and relapsed with the relaxing and retiring of the diaphragm; and it was thought that nothing but the loss of blood prevented pulsation from being restored. In the third experiment, the supra orbital nerve was touched, when the muscles of the face were thrown into frightful action and contortions. The scene was hideous; and many spectators left the room; and one gentleman nearly fainted, either from terror, or from the momentary sickness which the scene occasioned. In the fourth experiment, from meeting the electric power from the spinal marrow to the elbow, the fingers were put in motion, and the arm was agitated in such a manner, that it seemed to point to some spectators, who were dreadfully terrified, from an apprehension that the body was actually come to life.

From these experiments, Dr Ure seemed to be of the opinion, that had not incisions been made in the blood-vessels of the neck, and the spinal marrow been lacerated, the body of the criminal might have been restored to life.

Burning of Moscow

When the French army invaded Russia in 1812, and penetrated as far as Moscow, the Russians, thinking it more glorious to destroy the ancient capital of the Czars, than suffer it to harbour and protect an enemy, caused it to be burnt to the ground. On the 3rd of September, the fire commenced; but that part of the town called the White City, was preserved by the French, until four distinct explosions destroyed it, shook the whole city to its foundations, and proclaimed the salvation of Russia, in the final departure of the enemy. M. Labeaume, an officer in the French army, attached to the division commanded by the Viceroy of Italy, who was an eye-witness, gives a most animated picture of this dreadful scene of desolation.

'The most heart-rending scene,' says he, 'which my imagination had ever conceived, far surpassing the saddest story in ancient or modern history, now presented itself to my eyes. A great part of the population of Moscow, terrified at our arrival, had concealed themselves in cellars, or secret recesses of their houses. As the fire spread around, we saw them rushing in despair from their various asylums. They uttered no complaint, fear had rendered them dumb; and hastily snatching up their most precious effects, they fled before the flames. Others of greater sensibility, and actuated by the feelings of nature, saved only their parents or their infants, who were closely clasped in their arms. They were followed by their other children, running as fast as their little strength would permit, and with all the wildness of childish terror, vociferating the beloved name of mother! The old people, borne down by grief more than by age, had not sufficient power to follow their families, and expired near the houses in which they were born. The streets, the public places, and particularly the churches, were filled with these unhappy people, who, lying on the remains of their property, suffered even without a murmur. No cry, no complaint was heard. Both the conqueror and the conquered were equally hardened.

'The fire, whose ravages could not be restrained, soon reached the finest parts of the city. These palaces which had been admired for the beauty of their architecture, and the elegance of their furniture, were enveloped in the flames. Their magnificent fronts, ornamented with bas-reliefs and statues, fell with a dreadful crash on the fragments of the pillars which had supported them. The churches, which were covered with iron and lead, were likewise destroyed, and with them, those beautiful steeples which we had seen the night before covered with gold and silver. The hospitals too, which contained more than twelve thousand wounded, soon began to burn. This offered a dreadful and harrowing spectacle. Almost all these poor wretches perished. A few who still lingered were seen crawling, half burnt, amongst the smoking ruins; and others, groaning under the heaps of dead bodies, endeavoured in vain to extricate themselves from the horrible destruction that surrounded them.

'The next day, the different streets could no longer be distinguished, and the places on which the houses had stood were marked only be confused heaps of stones calcined and black. On whatever side we turned, we saw only ruin and flames. The fire raged as if it were fanned by some invisible power. The most extensive range of buildings seemed to kindle, to burn, and to disappear in an instant.

'How shall I describe the confusion and tumult, when permission was granted to pillage this great city! Soldiers, sutlers, and galley slaves eagerly ran through the streets, penetrated into the deserted palaces, and carrying away every thing that could gratify their avarice. Some covered themselves with stuffs richly worked with gold and silk; some were enveloped in beautiful and costly furs; while others dressed themselves in women's and children's pelisse; and even the galley-slaves concealed their rags under the most splendid habits of the court. The rest crowded into cellars, and forcing open the doors, drank to excess the most luscious wines, and carried off an immense booty. The flames obstructing the passage of the principal streets, often obliged them to retrace their steps. Thus, wandering from place to place, through an immense city, the avenues of which they did not know, they sought in vain to extricate themselves from the labyrinth of fire. The love of plunder induced our soldiers to brave every danger. They precipitated themselves into the flames; they waded in

blood, treading upon the dead bodies without remorse, whilst the ruins of houses, mixed with burning coals, fell thick on their murderous hands.

'About the dawn of day, I witnessed a spectacle at once affecting and terrible; a crowd of the miserable inhabitants, drawing upon some mean vehicles all that they had been able to save from the general conflagration. The soldiers having robbed them of their horses, the men and women were slowly and painfully dragging along their little carts, some of which contained an infirm mother, others a paralytic old man, and others the miserable wrecks of half consumed furniture. Children, half naked, followed these interesting groups. Affliction, to which their age is commonly a stranger, was impressed on their features: and when the soldiers approached them, they ran crying into the arms of their mothers.

'When the conflagration had ceased, many of the Muscovites who had sought refuge in the neighbouring forest, re-entered the city, where they sought in vain for their houses, or for shelter in the temples, which had also been consumed. The public walks presented a revolting spectacle: the ground was publicly strewed with dead bodies, and from many of the half burnt trees was suspended the body of an incendiary.'

The singular patriotism of sacrificing the city in order to subdue the enemy, actuated all ranks. A Russian servant, whose master had quitted Moscow on the entrance of the French, remained behind, and made frequent attempts to secrete himself in the house, which was then occupied by one of Bonaparte's chief officers of the etat major. He was frequently detected and dismissed, but at length was admitted, on pretence of taking care of the furniture and other property of his absent master. No sooner, however, had he fixed himself in his old quarters, than he was discovered making several ineffectual attempts to set the house on fire; and when interrogated as to his motive for such extraordinary conduct, coolly replied, that 'every thing around him was burning, and he did not see why his master's house should escape.' With a degree of lenity almost surprising in an enraged enemy, he was only thrust out of doors, discontented at his own want of success, and evidently considering his master and himself disgraced by not being permitted to partake of the general sacrifice.

True Greatness Of Soul

A grenadier in the Duke of Berwick's army, being taken marauding, was sentenced to die. His officers went in a body to the Duke, and represented to him, that the unhappy man was one of the bravest officers in the army. The duke, however, ordered the provost to do his duty. The grenadier was conducted to the place of punishment; but in the instant they were about to tie his hands, he found means to slip away, and concealed himself in the camp. The duke, informed of his escape, ordered that the provost should be hanged up in his stead. The provost threw himself at his feet, and protested his innocence, but all in vain – the inexorable duke ordered him to immediate execution. The concealed grenadier, being informed of this circumstance, with an exalted generosity of sentiment, instantly repaired to the duke – 'My lord,' said he, 'I am the criminal: I am informed that an innocent man is to die in my stead. As he had no hand in my escape, order him to be brought back; and I die content.' This greatness of soul instantly disarmed the general, and he pardoned them both.

Effects of Fear

I once read the most horrible story of some French travellers, who attempted to explore the vaults of the Egyptian pyramids, which revives some of those terrifying obstructions we sometimes meet with in disturbed dreams. These persons had already traversed an extensive labyrinth of chambers and passages; they were on their return, and had arrived at the most difficult part of it,– a very long and winding passage, forming a communication between two chambers: its opening was narrow and low;– the ruggedness of the floor, sides, and roof, rendered their progress slow and laborious,–and these difficulties increased rapidly as they advanced. The torch with which they had entered became useless, from the impossibility of holding it upright, as the passage diminished its height. Both its height and width at length, however, became so much contracted that the party was compelled to crawl on their bellies.

Their wandering in these interminable passages (for such, in their fatigue of body and mind, they deemed them) seemed to be endless. Their alarm was already great, and their patience exhausted, when the headmost of the party cried out, that he could discern a light at the end of the passage, at a considerable distance a-head, but that he could not advance any further, and that, in his efforts to press on, in hopes to surmount the obstacle without complaining, he had squeezed himself so far into the reduced opening, that he had now no longer sufficient strength even to recede! The situation of the party may be easily imagined; their terror was beyond direction or advice; while their leader, whether from terror or the natural effect of his situation, swelled so that, if it were before difficult, it was now impossible for him to stir from the spot he thus miserably occupied. One of the party, at this dreadful and critical moment, proposed, in the intense selfishness to which the feeling of danger reduces all, as the only means of escape from this horrible confinement,– this living grave, to cut in pieces the wretched being who formed the obstruction, and clear it by dragging the dismembered carcass piece-meal past them! He heard this dreadful proposal, and contracting himself with agony at the idea of his death, was reduced by a strong muscular spasm to his usual dimensions, and was dragged out, affording room for the party to squeeze themselves past over his prostrate body. The unhappy creature was suffocated in the effort, and was left behind a corpse!

Account Of A Wild Man

In the year 1774, a savage, or wild man, was discovered by the shepherds, who fed their flocks in the neighbourhood of the forest of Yuary. This man, who inhabited the rocks that lay near the forests, was very tall, covered with hair, like a bear, and nimble as the Hisars. His greatest amusement was to see the sheep running, and to scatter them; and he testified his pleasure at this sight by loud fits of laughter, but never attempted to hurt those innocent animals. When the shepherds let loose their dogs after him, he fled with the swiftness of an arrow, and never allowed the dogs to come too near him. One morning he came to the cottage of some workmen, and one of them endeavoured to get near him, and catch him by the leg, he laughed heartily, and then made his escape. He seemed to be about thirty years of age. As the forest in question is very extensive, and has a communication with vast woods that belong to the Spanish territory, it is natural to suppose, that this solitary creature had been lost in his infancy and had subsisted on herbs.

The Plague Of Locusts

A modern traveller relates the following phenomenon of the locust. We transcribe it as follows:—

'I was one day standing on the great battery, when, casting my eye toward the Barbary coast, I observed an odd sort of greenish cloud making to the Spanish shore; not, like other clouds, with rapidity or swiftness, but with a motion so slow, that sight itself was a long time before it would allow it such. At last, it came just over my head, and interposing between the sun and me, so thickened the air, that I lost the very sight of day. At this moment it reached the land; and though very near in imagination, it began to dissolve, and lose its first denseness; when, all on a sudden, there fell such a vast number of locusts, as exceeded the thickest storm of hail or snow that I had ever seen. All around me was immediately covered with those crawling creatures; and yet they continued to fall so thick, that with my cane I knocked down thousands. It is scarcely imaginable the havoc I made in a very short space of time; much less conceivable is the horrid desolation which attended the visitation of these animalculae. There was not, in a day of two's time, the least leaf to be seen on a tree, nor any green thing in a garden. Nature seemed buried in her own ruins; and the vegetable world to be supported only to be monument. I never saw the hardest winter, in those parts, attended with equal desolation. When, glutton-like, they had devoured all that should have sustained them, and the more valuable part of God's creation – whether weary with gorging, or over thirsty with devouring, I leave to the phi-losophers, – they made to ponds, brooks, and standing pools, and revenged their own rage upon nature upon their own vile carcasses; in every one of these you might see them lie in heaps like little hills, drowned indeed, and but attended with stenches so noisesome, that it gave the distracted neigh-bourhood too great reason to apprehend yet more fatal consequences. A pestilential infection is the dread of every place, but especially of all parts of the Mediterranean. The priests, therefore, repaired to a little chapel, built in the open fields, to be made use of on such like occasions, there to deprecate the cause of this dreadful visitation. In a week's time, or thereabouts, the stench was over, and every thing of verdant nature in its pristine order!'

Infection Strangely Communicated

In the year 1751, the grave-digger at Chelwood in Somersetshire opened a grave, wherein a man who had died of the small-pox had been interred about thirty years before. By the deceased's desire he had been buried in an oak coffin, which was so firm that it might have been taken out whole, but the gravedigger not choosing that, forced the spade through the lid, where there came forth such a stench, that he had never smelt the like before. It being a person of credit who was to be buried in the grave, the whole village attended the funeral, as well as many people from the neighbouring villages; and a few days after, about fourteen persons were seized in one day with the usual symptoms of the small-pox, and in three days more, every soul, but two, in the whole village, who had not had it, were seized in a like manner. Their disorder proved to be so favourable, that no more than two persons died of the whole number, which was about thirty, and one of them was a woman who came down stairs when the pock was at its height, and died the same night. The same disorder was carried all round the villages, by the country people who attended the funeral, and proved very favourable every where.

Attack Of A Fish

As Mr John Moffat, a stout and active young man, was lately crossing the Esk, on his return from his salmon stake-nets, he was closely pursued in the water by a fish of the shark species, which, after slightly biting his legs in above twenty different places, at last got the whole of his left leg transversely within its mouth. In this situation, Moffat seized the point of the fish's upper and lower jaw, and by violent effort extricated himself, and, making two or three rapid springs, got into shallow water. His leg was severely wounded in the place where it was seized across.

Setting In Of The Monsoon

The shades of evening (says Mr Forbes in his Oriental Memoirs,) approached us as we reached the ground, and just as the encampment was completed the atmosphere suddenly grew dark, the heat became oppressive, and an usual stillness presaged the immediate setting in of the monsoon. The whole appearance of nature resembled those solemn preludes to earthquakes and hurricanes in the West Indies, from which the east in general is providentially free. We were allowed very little time for conjecture: in a few minutes the heavy clouds burst over us.

I witnessed seventeen monsoons in India, but this exceeded them all, in its awful appearance and dreadful effects. Encamped in a low situation, on the borders of a lake, formed to collect the rising water, we found ourselves in a few hours in a liquid plain. The tentpins giving way, in a loose soil, the tents fell down, and left the whole army exposed to the contending elements. A hundred thousand human beings, with more than two hundred thousand elephants, camels, horses, and oxen, suddenly overwhelmed by this storm, in a strange country, without any knowledge of high or low ground, the whole being covered by an immense lake, and surrounded by thick darkness, which prevented our distinguishing a single object, except such as the vivid glare of lightning displayed in horrible forms. No language can describe the encampment thus instantaneously destroyed, and covered with water; amid the cries of old men and help-less women, terrified by the piercing shrieks of their expiring children, unable to afford them relief. During this dreadful night more than two hundred persons and three thousand cattle perished, and the morning dawn exhibited a shocking spectacle.

Such was the general situation of the army, such the condi-tion of the campaign. As secretary to the commanding officer, I was almost one of his family, and generally slept in his tent. At this time he was ill with a violent fever, and on the com-mencement of the storm had been removed in his palanquin to the village. I endeavoured to follow him; but up to my knees in water, and often plunging into holes much deeper, I was compelled to return to the tent; there being left alone, and perceiving the water gradually rising, I stood upon a chair, to keep above its surface; by midnight it had risen above three feet. The shrieks of the surrounding women and children, and the moaning of the cattle, especially of dying camels, were horrible. To increase my distress the pins gave way, and the tent fell on me, when no calls for assistance could be heard. Providentially it was a small Indian tent, with a centre pole, round which it clung; had it been the colonel's usual mar-quee, of English canvas, I must have been smothered. At last finding myself nearly exhausted, I determined to make one more effort for my deliverance, in which I happily succeeded. Guided through the lake by tremendous flashes of lightning, after many difficulties, I reached the hut whether they had conveyed the colonel, and there found the surgeon general, and several other gentlemen, drying their clothes around a large fire in the centre: with them I passed the remainder of this miserable night, among serpents, scorpions, and centipedes, which the fire within, and the heavy rain without, had driven from their hiding places. Several of our men were stung by the scorpions, and bit by snakes and centipedes; none fatally. The scorpion, though less dangerous than the malignant serpents, inflicts a wound which, like that of the centipedes, is attended with inflammation and fever; his sting at the end of the tail he darts with great force at the object of his fury; the latter bites by means of strong forceps at his mouth: this reptile is more common than the scorpion, and more easily concealed. If the scorpion is surrounded by flaming spirits or burning embers, and can find no egress, he stings himself to death.

Such was our night: the next morning the camp exhibited a scene of woe; the train of artillery was sunk several feet into the earth, and covered by the water. To convey them and the stores to Dhuboy required the utmost exertion, and, with the assistance of elephants, could not be accomplished in less than seven days, although only a distance of six miles.

Plagues Of Egypt

The following dreadful account of the plagues of Egypt, is extracted from Edward Daniel Clark's travels in Europe, Asia, and Africa.

The mercury in Fahrenheit's thermometer seemed at this time fixed. It remained at 90° for several days, without the smallest perceptible change. Almost every European suffered an inflammation of the eyes. Many were troubled with cutaneous disorders. The prickly heat was very common. This was attributed to drinking the muddy water of the Nile, the inhabitants having no other. Their mode of purifying it, in a certain degree, is by rubbing the inside of the water-vessels with bruised almonds: this precipitates a portion of the mud, but it is never quite clear. Many persons were afflicted with sores upon the skin, which were called 'Boils of the Nile;' and dysenterical complaints were universal. A singular species of lizard made its appearance in every chamber, having circular membranes at the extremity of its feet, which gave it such tenacity that it crawled upon panes of glass, or upon the surface of pendent mirrors. This revolting sight was common to every apartment, whether in the houses of the rich or the poor; at the same time, such a plague of flies covered all things over with their swarms, that it was impossible to eat without hiring persons to stand by every table with feathers or flappers, to drive them away. Liquor could not be poured into a glass; the mode of drinking was by keeping the mouth of every bottle covered until the moment it was applied to the lips; and instantly covering it with the palm of the hand, when removing it to offer to any one else. The utmost attention to cleanliness, by a frequent change of every article of wearing apparel, could not repel the attacks of the swarms of vermin which seemed to infest the air of the place. A gentleman made his appearance, before a party he had invited to dinner, completely covered with lice. The only explanation he could give as to the cause was, that he had sat for a short time in one of the boats upon the canal.

An Account Of An Uncommon Tempest

Mr Brydone, a late ingenious traveller, says in his account of Malta, that on the 29th of October, in the year 1757, about three quarters of an hour after midnight, there appeared to the south-west of the city, a great black cloud, which as it approached, changed its colour until at last it became like a flame of fire mixed with black smoke. A dreadful noise was heard on its approach, which alarmed the whole city. It passed over the port, and came first to an English ship, which in an instant was torn to pieces, and nothing left but the hulk; part of the masts, sails, and cordage, were carried along with the cloud at a considerable distance. The small boats that were in its way, were torn to pieces, or sunk; the noise increased, and became more frightful. A sentinel, terrified at its approach, took shelter in his box; both he and it were lifted up, and carried into the sea, where he perished; it traversed a considerable part of the city, and laid in ruins almost every thing in its course. Several houses were thrown down, nor was there any steeple left standing in its passage; the bells, with the spires of some, were carried to a considerable distance; the roofs of the houses were demolished and beat down, which, if it happened in the day-time, must have caused a dreadful slaughter, as the people would have all run to the churches. It went off at the north-east point of the city, and, demolishing the light-house, it is said to have mounted up into the air with a most frightful noise, and passed over the sea to Sicily, where it tore up some trees, and did other damage; but its force had been spent in Malta. The number killed and wounded, was near 200; and the loss of shipping, houses, and churches, was very considerable.

However the learned may differ in opinions concerning this singular phenomenon, the sentiments of the people are concise and positive; they declare with one voice, that it was a legion of devils let loose to punish them for their sins. There are a thousand persons in Malta, who will make oath that they saw them within the cloud, all as black as pitch, and breathing out fire and brimstone. They add, that if there had not been a few godly persons amongst them, the whole city would certainly have been involved in universal destruction.

The Dead Alive!

Some hypochondriacs have fancied themselves miserably afflicted in one way, and some in another; some have insisted that they were tea-pots, and some that they were town clocks; one that he was extremely ill, and another that he was actually dying. But perhaps none of this blue-devil class ever matched in extravagance a patient of the late Dr Stevenson, of Baltimore.

The hypochondriac, after ringing the change of every mad conceit that ever tormented a crazy brain, would have it at last that he was dead, actually dead. Dr Stevenson having been sent for one morning in great haste, by the wife of the patient, hastened to his bed-side, where he found him stretched out at full length, his hands across his breast, his toes in contact, his eyes and mouth closely shut, and his looks cadaverous.

'Well, sir, how do you do? how do you do, this morning?' asked Dr Stevenson, in a jocular way, approaching his bed. 'How do I do!' replied the hypochondriac, faintly, 'a pretty question to ask a dead man.' 'Dead!' replied the doctor. 'Yes, sir, quite dead; I died last night about twelve o'clock.'

Dr Stevenson, putting his hand gently on the forehead of the hypochondriac, as if to ascertain whether it was cold, and also feeling his pulse, exclaimed, in a doleful tone, 'Yes, the poor man is dead enough; 'tis all over with him, and now the sooner he can be buried the better.' Then stepping up to his wife, and whispering to her not to be frightened at the measures he was about to take, he called to the servant: 'My boy, your poor master is dead; and the sooner he can be put into the ground the better. Run to C——m, for I know he always keeps New England coffins by him ready made; and, do you hear, bring him a coffin of the largest size, for your master makes a stout corpse, and having died last night, and the weather being warm, he will not keep long.'

Away went the servant, and soon returned with a proper coffin. The wife and family, having got their lesson from the doctor, gathered around him, and howled not a little while they were putting the body in the coffin. Presently the pall-bearers, who were quickly provided, and let into the secret, started with the hypochondriac for the church-yard. They had not gone far before they were met by the one of the townspeople, who, having been properly drilled by Stevenson, cried out, 'Ah doctor, what poor soul have you got there?'

'Poor Mr B——,' sighed the doctor, 'left us last night.'

'Great pity he had not left us twenty years ago,' replied the other, 'he was a bad man.'

Presently another of the townsmen met them with the same question, 'And what poor soul have you got there, doctor?'

'Poor Mr B——,' answered the doctor again, 'is dead.'

'Yes, and to the bottomless pit,' said the other; 'for if he is not gone there, I see not what use there is for such a place.' Here the dead man bursting off the lid of the coffin, which had purposely been left loose, leaped out, exclaiming, 'O you villain! I am gone to the bottomless pit, am I? Well, I have come back again, to pay such ungrateful rascals as you are.' A chase was immediately commenced by the dead man after the living, to the petrifying consternation of many of the spectators, at the sight of a corpse, in all the horrors of the winding sheet, running through the streets. After having exercised himself in a copious perspiration by the fantastic race, the hypochondriac was himself brought home by Dr Stevenson, freed from all his complaints; and by strengthening food, generous wine, cheerful company, and moderate exercise, was soon restored to perfect health.

Malignant Vapour

The following melancholy event, which was caused by a fatal vapour, is narrated by Dr Comor, and may be relied upon as a fact.

As some persons were digging in a cellar in Paris, for supposed hidden treasures, the maid went down to call up her master, and found them all dead, but in their working postures, and seemingly intent on their several offices, one digging, another shovelling away the earth, &c. The wife of one of them was sat down by the side of a hopper, leaning her head on her hands, as if weary and thoughtful. All of them, in short, appeared in their natural postures and actions, with their eyes wide open, but as stiff as statues, and as cold as clay.

A House Struck With Lightning

The following account of a house struck by lightning, at Russing-End, near Hitchen, in Hertfordshire, is related by an eye-witness:–

'About one o'clock, on Wednesday, June 26th, 1771, I was going into my hay-field, and perceived a black storm rising in the south in direct opposition to the wind, when it was full north: it continued hanging there for a full hour, and not seeming to come on, I walked into my field which was about half a mile off; on my arriving there a violent clap of thunder came, through the sun at that time shone very clear. I turned about to go home, and thinking it would rain hard proceeded to go through a wood; but on getting into the middle of it, as I heard no continuance of the thunder, I imagined the storm was over, but as I was returning I heard a second clap, which was accompanied by a slight sprinkling of rain. I then continued my walk through the wood into a field, and looking towards the black cloud saw a small flash of lightning succeeded by a pale spiral pillar of fire, which shot up into the clear air a vast height, then followed a loud clap of thunder; from these circumstances I imagined some mischief had happened in the neighbourhood. On my coming into the house I looked at the clock, and found it wanted five minutes of three; it then rained very fast. The next day I was told that much damage was done at a farm house at Russing-End. I went there and found the accident had happened just after their clock struck three. I was shewn the back part of it, and a large chimney, to which a small bed-chamber chimney was fastened by an iron square cramp and an iron hook, which I imagine attracted the lightning: it entirely took down the chimney as if done by a workman. At the back was a leaden gutter, and an oak board to support it; neither of which were moved or discoloured: from thence it broke a hole on the left-hand side of the chimney, and the chimney being stopped up where it is usual to have chimney boards, it diverted its course to the right of the closet, containing several bottles of liquor, all the full bottles were broke, the empty ones saved; it forced open the closet door though locked, and covered it all over with brimstone; it forced off the two middle ledges, the upper and lower ones remaining firm; from thence it descended into the kitchen, and ran over two spits on the rack, covering them with a yellowish slime and of a clammy feel; it then broke to pieces a cupboard under them, in which was a brass tobacco-box full of gunpowder, the lid of which it blew open without firing the gunpowder, but only mixing it with a yellowish colour; a bird, which hung on the bacon rack, six feet off the chimney, was not hurt, only a splinter two feet long forced itself into his cage; the panels of the cupboard were flung to the farther end of the kitchen; a woman and a child who sat near the window, were flung out of their chairs unhurt; but the maid, who was sweeping the house near the door which was open, was beaten down senseless, and laid so till ten o'clock that night; her face and all her right side were scorched, but her clothes not singed at all: it discoloured a tin candle-box, without firing either the candles or the matches; it run over a chopping knife which hung in the chimney, and from thence made a black streak in the fire-place across the hearth; it made a small hole into the yard through the wall of the house, under the window shutter, and broke a hole in the shutter a foot above it; wherever there were nails in the window lights it melted the lead all about it; some brass candlesticks were spotted in many places with blue spots burnt in, they were underneath a shelf of teacups which were untouched: it went out of the door obliquely into the table, and passed under the horses' bellies without harm, but so terrified them, that they would not feed for the remainder of the day; it struck a colt blind which was in an adjoining field, set fire to a hay rick, killed three pigs, and otherwise done much damage.'

Remarkable Circumstances

In the month of September, 1824, the body of a young women, dressed in black silk, with a watch, a ring, and a small sum of money, was found floating near Spithead, by a lieutenant of the impress, and conveyed to Ryde in the Isle of Wight. As no person owned it, a parish officer, who was also an undertaker, took upon himself to inter the body, for the property that was attached to it, which was accordingly performed.

One evening, about a fortnight after the event, a poor man and woman were seen to come into the village, and on application to the undertaker for a view of the property which belonged to the unfortunate drowned person, they declared it to have been their daughter, who was overset in a boat when she was going to Spithead to see her husband. They also wished to pay whatever expense the undertaker had been at, and to receive the trinkets, &c. which had so lately been the property of one so dear to them: but this the undertaker would by no means consent to. They repaired, therefore, to the churchyard, where, the woman having prostrated herself at the grave of the deceased, continued sometime in silent meditation, or prayer; then crying, Pillilew! After the manner of the Irish at funerals, she sorrowfully departed with her husband.

The curiosity of the inhabitants of Ryde, excited by the first appearance and behaviour of this couple, was changed into wonder, when returning, in less than three weeks, they accused the undertaker of having buried their daughter without a shroud! saying, she had appeared in a dream, complaining of the mercenary and sacrilegious undertaker, and lamenting the indignity, which would not let her spirit rest!

The undertaker stoutly denied the charge. But the woman having secretly purchased a shroud (trying it on herself), at Upper Ryde, was watched by the seller, and followed about twelve o'clock at night into the church-yard. After lying a short time on the grave, she began to remove the mould with her hands, and, incredible as it may seem, by two o'clock she had uncovered the coffin, which with much difficulty, and the assistance of her husband, was lifted out of the grave. On opening it, the stench was almost intolerable, and stopped the operation for some time; but, after taking a pinch of snuff, she gently raised the head of the deceased, taking from the back of it, and the bottom of the coffin, not a shroud but a dirty piece of flannel, with part of the hair sticking to it, and which the writer saw lying in the hedge so lately as the middle of the present year. Clothing the body with the shroud, every thing was carefully replaced; and, on the second application, the undertaker, overwhelmed with shame, restored the property. The woman (whose fingers were actually worn to the bone with the operation) retired with her husband, and has never been heard of since.

A Nocturnal Ramble

The following remarkable instance of a boy walking in his sleep, was recently related in the Westmoreland Advertiser.

A boy, in the service of Mr Thomas Fawcett, of Gate, lately accompanied his master in shooting all day upon the moors; and on returning in the evening, his master desired him to make the best of his way home. The boy proceeded on foot, but being much fatigued, sat down, and fell asleep. How long he remained in that situation was uncertain, as, when found, he was in his own bed, asleep; and a neighbour, passing on the road early next morning, found his clothes scattered in various directions, nearly half a mile off. The account he gave was, that he dreamed he had been at a neighbour's house, at a good supper, after which he supposed he went to bed there. It appears he actually walked three miles, though in a profound sleep the whole time; during which he stripped off his clothes, and walked home naked, passed the gate, and went up stairs to bed, being the whole of the time asleep.

Sympathy Of The Horse

The following singular instance of sympathy in the horse occurred some time since:– A Mr Allix had been out coursing, and, approaching home, enquired the hour of his servant;

on being informed, he remarked that there was time for a
short ride before dinner, turned his horse about, took a cir-
cuit, and again arrived within about half a mile of his own
house, when the servant observed him to be gradually falling from his horse, pointing at the same time to the ground.
The servant got up in time to catch his master in his arms,
and having laid him on the ground, a game-keeper, who was
passing by, staid with Mr Allix until the servant went to the
house for assistance. He soon after returned on a valuable
horse. On the approach of the animal, he smelt to his master
(apparently a lifeless corpse), snorted, ran back a few paces,
fell on his side, and died instantly!

Violent Storm

On August 26, 1823, at three o'clock in the afternoon, the
sudden heat of the atmosphere announced an approaching
storm, which shewed itself coming from the S.E. over the
village of Boncourt, and not far from there a remarkable
water spout made its appearance. Its base touched the earth,
and its summit was lost in the clouds. It was formed of a
dense dark vapour, and flames darted frequently through its
centre. In its course onwards, it tore up or broke the trees for
the space of a league, destroying between seven and eight
hundred trees, and at length burst with vast impetuosity on
the village of Marchefroy, destroying in one instant the half
of the houses. The walls were shaken to the foundations,
and crumbled down in every direction; they were torn off
and split, and the pieces carried away half a league by the
force of the wind. Some of the inhabitants who remained
in the village were knocked down and wounded; those at
work in the fields, fortunately the greater number, were also
thrown down by the violence of the storm, which destroyed

the harvest, and wounded or killed the beasts. Hail-stones as big almost as a man's fist, stones and other bodies, showered down by this impetuous wind, wounded several individuals very severely. Waggons heavily laden were broken in pieces, and their burdens dispersed. Axle-trees capable of supporting the weight of eight or ten tons were broken, and large wheels were carried two or three hundred paces from where the storm found them. One of the wagons, almost entire, was even carried over a brick-kiln, some portions of which were carried to a considerable distance. A steeple, several hamlets, and isolated houses, and new walls were blown down, and other villages were considerably damaged.

Singular Death

On the 8th of August, 1823, a young man, named Thomas Clements, lost his life in a manner as dreadful as it was extraordinary. He was fishing with a draw net, near Elizabeth Castle, Jersey, and taking a little sole out of the net, he put it between his teeth to kill it, when the fish, with a sudden spring, forced itself into his throat, and choked him. The unfortunate man had just time to call for assistance, but it came too late; he expired soon after in dreadful agony.

Dreadful Sufferings Of Lieutenant Spearing

The following remarkable account of the sufferings of Lieutenant George Spearing, who lived seven days in a coal-pit, without any sustenance, except some rain-water, was related by himself in a letter to the public Journals of the time, and may be relied upon as authentic.

'On Wednesday, September 13th, 1769, between three and four o'clock in the afternoon, I went into a little wood called Northwoodside (situated between two and three miles to the N.W. of Glasgow), with a design to gather a few hazel-nuts. I think that I could not have been in the wood more than a quarter of an hour, nor have gathered more than ten nuts, before I unfortunately fell into an old coal-pit, exactly seventeen yards deep, which had been made through a solid rock. I was some little time insensible. Upon recovering my recollection, I found myself sitting nearly as a tailor does at his work, the blood flowing pretty fast from my mouth; and I thought that I had broken a blood vessel, and consequently had not long to live; but, to my great comfort, I soon discovered that the blood proceeded from a wound in my tongue, which I suppose I had bitten in my fall. Looking at my watch (it was ten minutes past four), and getting up, I surveyed my limbs, and to my inexpressible joy found that not one was broken. I was soon reconciled to my situation, having from my childhood thought that something very extraordinary was to happen to me in the course of my life; and I had not the least doubt of being relieved in the morning; for the wood being but small and situated near a populous city, it is much frequented, especially in the nutting season, and there are several foot-paths leading through it.

'Night now approached, when it began to rain, not in gentle showers, but in torrents of water, such as is generally experienced at the autumnal equinox. The pit I had fallen into was about five feet in diameter; but, not having been worked for several years, the subterranean passages were choked up, so that I was exposed to the rain, which continued with very small intermissions, till the day of my release; and, indeed, in a very short time, I was completely wet through. In this comfortless situation I endeavoured to take some repose. A forked stick that I found in the pit, and which I placed diagonally to the side of it, served alternately to support my head as a pillow, and my body occasionally, which was much bruised; but in the whole time I remained here, I do not think that I ever slept one hour together. Having passed a very disagreeable and tedious night, I was somewhat cheered by the appearance of day-light, and the melody of a robin redbreast that had perched directly over the mouth of the pit; this pretty little warbler continued to visit my quarters every morning of my confinement; which I construed into a happy omen of my future deliverance; and I sincerely believe the trust I had in Providence, and the company of this little bird, contributed much to the serenity of mind I constantly enjoyed to the last. At the distance of about a hundred yards, in a direct line from the pit, there was a water-mill. The miller's house was nearer to me, and the road to the mill still nearer. I could frequently hear the horses going this road to and from the mill; frequently I heard human voices; and I could distinctly hear the ducks and hens about the mill. I made the best use of my voice on every occasion; but it was to no purpose; for the wind, which was constantly high, blew in a direct line from the mill to the pit, which easily accounts for what I heard; and at the same time my voice was carried the contrary way. I cannot say I suffered much from hunger. After two or three days that appetite ceased; but my thirst was intolerable: and, though it constantly rained, yet I could not till the third or fourth day preserve a drop of it, as the earth at the bottom of my pit sucked it up as fast as it ran down. In this distress I sucked my clothes; but from them I could extract but little moisture. The shock I received in the fall, together with the dislocation of one of my ribs, kept me, I imagine, in a continual fever; I cannot otherwise account for my suffering so much more from thirst than I did from hunger. At last I discovered the thigh-bone of a bull (which I afterwards heard had fallen into the pit about eighteen years before me), almost covered in earth. I dug it up; and the large end

of it left a cavity that, I suppose, might contain a quart. This the water drained into, but so very slowly, that it was a considerable time before I could dip a nut-shell full at a time; which I emptied into the palm of my hand, and so drank it. The water began now to increase pretty fast, so that I was glad to increase my reservoir, insomuch, that on the fourth or fifth day, I had a sufficient supply; and this water was certainly the preservation of my life.

'At the bottom of the pit there were great quantities of reptiles, such as frogs, toads, large black snails, or slugs, &c. These noxious creatures would frequently crawl about me, and often got into my reservoir; nevertheless I thought it the sweetest water I had ever tasted. I have frequently taken both frogs and toads out of my neck, where I suppose they took shelter while I slept. The frogs I carefully preserved, as I did not know but I might be under the necessity of eating them, which I should not have scrupled to have done had I been very hungry.

Saturday the 16th, there fell but little rain, and I had the satisfaction to hear the voices of some boys in the wood. Immediately I called out with all my might, but it was all in vain, though I afterwards learned that they actually heard me: but, being prepossessed with an idle story of a wild man being in the wood, they ran away affrighted.

Sunday, the 17th, was my birth-day, when I completed my forty-first year, and I think some of my acquaintance, having accidentally heard that I had gone the way I did, sent two or three porters out purposefully to search the pits for me. These men went to the miller's house, and made inquiry for me; but, on account of the very great rain at the time, they never entered the wood, but cruelly returned to their employers, telling them they had searched the pit, and that I was not to be found. Many people in my dismal situation would, no doubt, have died with despair; but, I thank God, I enjoyed a perfect serenity of mind; so much so, that on Tuesday afternoon, and when I had been six nights in the pit, I very composedly, by way of amusement, combed my wig on my knee, humming a tune, and thinking of Archer in the 'Beaux Stratagem.'

At length the morning (Sept 20), the happy morning for my deliverance came. Through the brambles and bushes that covered the mouth of the pit, I could discover the sun shining bright, and my pretty warbler was chanting his melodious strains, when my attention was roused by a confused noise of human voices, which seemed to be approaching fast towards the pit; immediately I called out, and most agreeably surprised several of my acquaintances, who were in search of me. They told me that they had not the most distant hope of finding me alive; but wished to give my body a decent burial, should they be so fortunate as to find it. As soon as they heard my voice, they all ran towards the pit, and I could distinguish a well-known voice exclaim, 'Good God! he is still living!' Another of them, though a very honest North

Briton, betwixt his surprise and joy, could not help asking me, in the Hibernian style, if I were still alive? I told him I was, and hearty too; and then gave them particular directions how to proceed in getting me out. Fortunately at that juncture a collier, from a working pit in the neighbourhood, was passing along the road, and hearing an unusual noise in the wood, his curiosity prompted him to learn the occasion. By his assistance, and a rope from the mill, I was soon safely landed on terra firma. The miller's wife had very kindly brought some milk warm from the cow; but, on my coming into the fresh air, I grew rather faint and could not taste it. Need I be ashamed to acknowledge, that the first dictates of the heart prompted me to fall on my knees, and ejaculate a silent thanksgiving to the God of my deliverance.

Every morning while I was in the pit, I tied a knot in the corner of my handkerchief, supposing that, if I died there, and my body should be afterwards found, the number of knots would certify how many days I had lived. Almost the first question my friends asked me was, how long had I been in the pit? Immediately I drew out my handkerchief, and bade them count the knots. They found seven, the exact number of nights I had been there. We now hastened out of the wood. I could walk without support; but that was not allowed, each person present striving to shew me how much they were rejoiced that they had found me alive and so well. They led me to the miller's house, where a great number of people were collected to see me. A gentleman, who had a country house just by, very kindly, at my request, sent for a glass of white wine. I ordered a piece of bread to be toasted, which I soaked in the wine, and ate. I now desired the miller's wife to make me up a bed, fondly thinking that nothing more was wanting than a little refreshing in terminate my misfortune. But alas! I was still to undergo greater sufferings than I had yet endured.

By the almost continual rains, together with the cold damp arising from the wet ground on which I laid, and not being able to take the least exercise to keep up a proper circulation of the blood, my legs were much swelled and benumbed. Some of my friends, observing this, proposed to send to Glasgow for medical advice. I at first declined it, and happy had it been for me had I pursued my own inclinations; but unfortunately for me a physician and surgeon were employed, both of them ignorant of what ought to have been done. Instead of ordering my legs into cold water, or rubbing them with a coarse towel, to bring on a gradual circulation, they applied hot bricks and large poultices to my feet. This by expanding the blood-vessels too suddenly, put me to much greater torture than I have ever endured in my life, and not only prevented me enjoying that refreshing sleep I so much wanted, but actually produced a mortification in both my feet. I do not mean, by relating this circumstance, to reflect on the faculty in general at Glasgow; for I was afterwards attended by gentlemen who are an honour to the profession. The same method was pursued for several days, without even giving me bark till I mentioned it myself. This happily stopped the progress of the mortification, which the doctors did not know had taken place till the miller's wife shewed them a black spot, about as broad as a shilling, at the bottom of my left heel. In a day or two more the whole skin, together with all the nails of my left foot, and three from my right, came off like the fingers of a glove.

'I continued six weeks at the miller's, when the roads became too bad for the doctors to visit me, so that I was under necessity of being carried in a sedan chair to my lodgings in Glasgow. By this time my right foot was quite well; but in my left, where the above mentioned black spot appeared, there was a large wound, and it too plainly appeared that the os calcis was nearly all decayed; for the surgeon could put his probe through the centre of it. The flesh too at the bottom of my foot was quite separated from the bones and tendons, so that I was forced to submit to have it cut off. In this painful state I lay for several months, reduced to a mere skeleton, taking thirty drops of laudanum every night; and though it somewhat eased the pain in my foot, it was generally three or four in the morning before I got any rest. My situation now became truly alarming: I had a consultation of surgeons, who advised me to wait with patience for an exfoliation, when they had not the least doubt but that they should soon cure my foot. At the same time they candidly acknowledged that it was impossible to ascertain the precise time when that would happen, as it might be six or even twelve months, before it came to pass. In my emaciated condition I was certain that it was not possible for me to hold out half the time; and knowing that I must be a very great cripple with the loss of my heel-bone, I came to the determined resolution to have my leg taken off, and appointed the very next day for the operation; but no surgeon came near me. I sincerely believe they wished to perform a cure; but being, as I thought, the best judge of my own feelings, I was resolved this time to be guided by my own opinion; accordingly, on the 2nd of May, 1770, my leg was taken off a little below the knee.

Yet, notwithstanding I had so long endured the rod of affliction, misfortunes still followed me. About three hours after the amputation had been performed, and when I was quiet in bed, I found myself nearly fainting with the loss of blood; the ligatures had all given way, and the arteries had bled a considerable time before it was discovered. By this time the wound was inflamed; nevertheless I was under the necessity of once more submitting to the operation of the needle, and the principal artery was sewed up four different times before the blood was stopped. I suffered much for two or three days, not daring to take a wink of sleep; for, the moment I shut my eyes, my stump (though constantly held by the nerve), would take such convulsive motions, that I really think a stab to the heart could not be attended with greater pain. My blood too was become so very poor and thin, that it absolutely drained through the wound near a fortnight after my leg was cut off. I lay for eighteen days and nights in one position, not daring to move lest the ligature should again give way; but I could endure it no longer, and ventured to turn myself in bed, contrary to the advice of my surgeon, which I happily effected, and never felt greater pleasure in my life. Six weeks after the amputation, I went out in a sedan chair for the benefit of the air, being exactly nine months from the day I fell into the pit. Soon after I took lodgings in the country; where getting plenty of warm new milk, my appetite and strength increased daily; and I ever after enjoyed perfect health, and have since been the father of nine children.

Tales from the Terrific Register
The Book of Murder

EDITED BY CATE LUDLOW

978 07524 5266 1

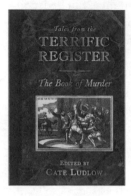

Including 'the horrible murder of a child by starvation', dreadful executions, foul tortures and one of the earliest mentions of a now notorious killer who turned his victims into pies, this selection of gruesome tales will chill all but the sturdiest of hearts. Many of these tales have not appeared in print since Charles Dickens himself read them. Illustrated with original woodcuts, it will fascinate anyone with an interest in true crime.

Tales from the Terrific Register
The Book of London

EDITED BY CATE LUDLOW

978 07524 5264 7

Fast-paced and astonishingly gory, the *Terrific Register* was a publishing sensation. As a schoolboy, Charles Dickens was never without a copy. This selection contains many tales of London life that will startle the modern reader. Including gripping stories of fires, floods and disasters, 'eye-witness' accounts of the great plague and 'the last moment of Lord Balmerino, executed on Tower Hill, 1746', it is a fascinating read.

Visit our website and discover thousands of other History Press books.
www.thehistorypress.co.uk